Guided Meditations For Deep Sleep, Relaxation, Anxiety & Depression (2 in 1):

20+ Hours Of Positive Affirmations, Hypnosis, Scripts & Breathwork For Self-Love, Overthinking, Insomnia & Energy Healing

By Self-Healing Mindfulness Academy

10 Guided Meditations For Anxiety:

Positive Affirmations, Hypnosis, Scripts & Breathwork For Panic Attacks, Depression, Relaxation, Deep Sleep, Overthinking & Self-Love

By Self-Healing Mindfulness Academy

© Copyright 2021 - All rights reserved.

The content contained within this book may not be reproduced, duplicated or transmitted without direct written permission from the author or the publisher.
Under no circumstances will any blame or legal responsibility be held against the publisher, or author, for any damages, reparation, or monetary loss due to the information contained within this book; either directly or indirectly.

Legal Notice:
This book is copyright protected. This book is only for personal use. You cannot amend, distribute, sell, use, quote or paraphrase any part, or the content within this book, without the consent of the author or publisher.

Disclaimer Notice:
Please note the information contained within this document is for educational and entertainment purposes only. All effort has been executed to present accurate, up to date, and reliable, complete information. No warranties of any kind are declared or implied. Readers acknowledge that the author is not engaging in the rendering of legal, financial, medical or professional advice.

Table of Contents

Introduction: 5

Positive Affirmations: 8

Guided Meditations for Panic attacks 22

Meditation for Depression 28

Meditation for Relaxation 34

Meditation for Deep Sleep: 39

Meditations for Overthinking 44

Meditations for Self-Love 52

Meditation for Trust 57

Meditation for Patience 66

Meditation for Self-Awareness and Preservation 73

Introduction:

Meditation is a practical tool to still the mind, and to experience consciousness. Consciousness is the deepest layer of ones ability to understand, grasp and attract.

When the eternal lake of consciousness is quiet and still, Meditation can help with that, than one becomes aware of ones true nature.

Daily Meditation keeps a quiet mind, and resources the still lake of consciousness for a higher and eternal purpose.

All purposes which are fulfilled by the ocean can also be fulfilled by a small well.

Sit still, properly and attentive. The spine is upright, on flat on the ground on a mat.

These meditations can be practiced while sitting, or laying in an awake state, for best results find yourself facing North.

Be comfortable and have a meditative space around you, with least distraction. Only when the nature is still, attraction and abundance can be tapped into.

From the natural Peripherie we start our meditative journey to the personal nature.

This nature is essentially eternal, and full of abundance.

This abundance comes in energy and with quality. It has character as well as form and personality.

Be aware of this present situation and breathe. Gently in and out again, equal and aware, every breath is likewise streaming into the nose, and out again. Loosen the muscles on the shoulders, and neck, and open up the chest with a straight posture.

The life air is flowing into the nostrils and reaching the heart. Here, all meditation happens.

The heart is the spiritual abode of personality and bliss, everlasting wisdom and eternity.

Be aware of the breath touching the heart and notice it streaming out again. This process of conscious breathing keeps the focus on the subject matter.

The subject of personality is connected to a sense of self, or ego, which naturally expresses a desire. One is just aware of this thought, whatever it may be.

This is the matter of the mind, and the senses, knowing very well that there is coming and going of the breath.

Notice the duality of in- and out of the breathing. Are both equal?
Inhale one... two... three... four, exhale one... two... three... four. Pause for a moment.

Imagine sitting on a still lake of consciousness. The moon is shining in full and the light is reflected very authentically. This still lake receives the light of the moon very nicely, and hence the lake is still, the light can shine through the surface onto the ground of the lake.

The light is both reflected by the still lake of consciousness and touched deeply to the ground of the unconscious. Both, subtly are reached and pervaded by crystal clear moonlight.

This purity shall help us to be aware, therefore the meditations are dedicated to clean the mirror of the heart, which is full of material dust.

Through conscious breath the mirror can be cleaned and on can see the truth within. Natural desires and thoughts are arising, equally as the breathing arises and passes.

Everything, like ebb and flood comes and goes, but what we have attracted is still present with us. Therefore, we use a special technique of meditation to reduce the mind-clutter and to make space for pure attraction.

Purity comes in form of a person to you. The Person is the Highest Person, and Absolute Truth. Situated in the temple of the heart lingering on the lake of consciousness. This Absolute Truth is sitting on nice patio, with a beautiful seat made of softest cushion gras. The Supreme Person is clothed in silk and finest wool, decorated with abundant jewels, amulets, golden bangles and a beautiful flower garland.

This highest Supreme Person is the source of all abundance and attraction. The name of this person is Krishna, which means the all-attractive one. All-attractive. So whatever you can imagine, whatever you have ever dreamed of, whatever is possible and impossible is granted through the permission of this Highest Person.

The Supreme Personality sits within the heart of every living being, and one can address this spiritual state as follows:

'O, Supreme Attractor, please grant me access to the realm of consciousness where all is possible. I am hungry for attraction and abundance. Please allow me a bite of this transcendental joy and bliss. May all beings be happy.'

Contemplate, and breathe. Sit comfortably and stay in this consciousness for a moment. Become aware of the stillness of the lake, and just notice the mind focusing its intention to the longing for purity.

Breathe, and just accept this moment as it is, the Supreme Personality shall hear and listen.

For a moment, come to ease and listen to the matter of the breathing, how it is still present, knowing to be alive.

Give thanks and gratitude to the present moment, in mind, word and action. Fold your palms together, in front of the chest and be aware of the subtle energetic currents flowing from the palms and along the arms, shoulders, neck, head and heart.

By approaching the Supreme reservoir of all attraction has direct access to unlimited resources. This resource comes in form of conscious waves of energy.

Prepare and be aware, whatever you like to attract is just a connection. Not so far away, but the more precious and kindly we ask, the better one can receive.

Open the hands and palms facing upwards. This gesture helps to let go of unwanted and unnecessary clutter in mind and energy. Just surrender and let your palms face to the sky. Breathe equally, and relax. Everything is fine, we are just about to clean the mirror of the heart and mind which simple sounds.

<u>How to write your own meditations</u>

It is the best practice, writing and manifesting a piece of selflessness. Just pick out a pen, or notepad and write.

Whatever it is, as soon as you let go, it becomes meditative. Stilling the mind comes from the heart, and through writing one expresses the heart, along the arm to the fingertips onto the paper.

Give it a try and benefit from it, a whole life long this practice can bring long lasting attraction, of all the hearts desires.

Positive Affirmations:

Affirmation & Prayer for Attraction

Prayer has since worked and relieved people. Shamans, nature man, from all over the world have attracted wonders and forces to helped the tribe, like in the Mongolian desert, a Shaman sang with his tribe for relief. Rituals of dance and sacrifice were done. However, eventually, the Shaman fell into deep wishful prayer, finally attracting the rain.
Same stories are heard from all over the world. Deep, intentional prayer can send out a message of change, and actually transform a circumstance immediately.
Let's affirm and trust in the words, which shall attract all good things. Notably, all activities towards speaking, singing and praying are auspicious when used consciously and with humility.
Writing is a wonderful base of speaking, praying or reciting, therefore it deserves a special thanks. Giving it a proper place, writing will be discussed in later sections about attractive actions.
Attractive words include words that are full of worth and value. Praise, Glorification, Personal Truth, even abstract thoughts and ideas hold value. Words of highest order, are attracting pure results like love, bliss and joy.
'Today, I shall not worry, just for now, I shall be happy.'

' Just now, you shall be joyful, happy and at peace!'
'May all living beings be happy.'
Very mellow and subtle, these affirmations actually work wonders. Happiness and joy can be so easily attracted, especially in times of grief, anger, frustration, pain, and so on. Love functions through the space-time and is a universal force, stronger than any other force. Likewise, it emanates from within the heart and radiates. Therefore, try it out. Speak it and feel. Loud, or soft. Play with it.
Most importantly: Mean it. Truthfully.
Praising a loved one is also giving results very easily.
'You have done this very nicely!' 'Well done!'

' We are a good team!'

Positivity can uplift everyone to a mood swing, giving the truth with love and compassionate holds endless value. Truth spoken without compassion has no effect. Therefore, affirm it and mean it. Practice it, and be aware of voice, tone, and body language. Feel it and play with it.
To glorify is a good tool to enchant a personality that is worth of glorification. In most religions God is glorified, in natural tribes the weather entities are glorified, in simple means, one can even glorify ones cooking gear. Actually, in India there is one day in the year where all the utensils, from plates, to tables, to other things are glorified. This is to show respect for their service.

' O my beloved tea cup, I behold you to truly nurture me with kindness and a relief from today's stress.'
'O beloved rain clouds, I glorify the water you give us, so the crops can grow into a fruitful harvest.'

'Dear loved one, just one glance at your glorious form creates a smile of peace within my heart.'
Like this, one can practice this and really embrace the feeling, full of love and devotion. Really, life is emotional, life is fluid and ecstatic, however we live it. Say these words even to yourself. Making clear, appreciation attracts self- confidence.
'I am the Light of the World, You are the Light of the World, We are the Light of the World.'

Sing it, dance to it, be like an over- confident child, that is somewhat proud and boasting of energy. It gives strength and power.
Affirmations also work on the personal level, speaking truth about and personally to oneself.
'I feel...'
'I want to attract...'
'I am happy as I am, or even so, unhappiness cannot limit me.'

Let it be personal and stress your individuality, knowing to be part of the whole. We are all unique, yet different. This is the basic and personal truth of behaviour and philosophy.
Directly, one can also boost confidence, compassion, peace, and relationships by wording affirmations according to ones needs.
'Today, I speak truly and attract truth.'
'Now, I shall find happiness and attract happiness around me.'
'Let there be peace in every word I say.'
'May I trust the people around me, with compassion and kindness.'
'May I trust in the Law of Attraction, Light and Love.'

The universal force of Love is all-pervading like a constant, yet fine element, like the sky, love is everywhere, pervading everything. Trust in it. It is all-good.

Joyful affirmations

This is a mantra meditation. The joyful affirmations can be repeated silently in your head or spoken out loud. Try to really connect with the meaning behind the words.

May All the Joy be with All
May all the love be with all
May all the happiness be with all
Love, Peace & Harmony
May all the Joy be with Us
May all the love be with Us
May all the happiness be with us.
Love, Peace & Harmony
May all the Joy be with You
May all the Love be with you
May all the happiness be with you
Love, Peace & Harmony

May all the Joy be with me
May all the love be with me
May all the happiness be with me
Love, Peace & Harmony

I am the Joy of the World
I am the joy of the world
I am I am I am the joy of the world

You are the joy of the world
You are the joy of the world
You are, you are, you are the joy of the world

We are the joy of the world
We are the joy of the world
We are, we are, we are, the joy of the world.

Love, Joy and Harmony
Peace in Unity
Satisfaction
Love Attraction
Joy and Harmony,
Peace in Unity
Satisfaction

Affirming with Mantra:

Mantra is a special form of affirmation and meditation. It comes from the word manas meaning 'the mind' and tra meaning 'a tool to still or pacify'. One can receive a Mantra through a teacher or discipleship, receiving with it the full potential of the source or sacred sounds.

Mantra is also sung or recited. Like a motto or slogan, one can truly feel the intensity through repetition. There are special mantras like the Maha-mantra. The great teacher of meditation Srila Prabhupada gives a purport on the MAHA-Mantra:

The transcendental vibration established by the chanting of Hare Krsna, Hare Krsna, Krsna Krsna, Hare Hare/ Hare Rama, Hare Rama, Rama Rama, Hare Hare is the sublime method of reviving our Krsna consciousness. As living spiritual souls we are all originally Krsna conscious entities, but due to our association with matter from time immemorial, our consciousness is now polluted by the material atmosphere.

The material atmosphere, in which we are now living, is called maya, or illusion. Maya means "that which is not." And what is this illusion? The illusion is that we are all trying to be lords of material nature, while actually we are under the grip of her stringent laws. When a servant artificially tries to imitate the all-powerful master, this is called illusion. In this polluted concept of life, we are all trying to exploit the resources of material nature, but actually we are becoming more and more entangled in her complexities. Therefore, although we are engaged in a hard struggle to conquer nature, we are ever more dependent on her.

This illusory struggle against material nature can be stopped at once by revival of our Krsna consciousness. Krsna consciousness is not an artificial imposition on the mind; this consciousness is the original energy of the living entity. When we hear the transcendental vibration, this consciousness is revived. And this process is recommended for this age by authorities. By practical experience also, one can perceive that by chanting this maha-mantra, or the Great Chanting for Deliverance, one can at once feel a transcendental ecstasy coming through from the spiritual stratum. And when one is factually on the plane of spiritual understanding—surpassing the stages of senses, mind, and intelligence—one is situated on the transcendental plane. This chanting of Hare Krsna, Hare Krsna, Krsna Krsna, Hare Hare/ Hare Rama, Hare Rama, Rama Rama, Hare Hare is directly enacted from the spiritual platform, and thus this sound vibration surpasses all lower strata of consciousness—namely sensual, mental, and intellectual.

There is no need, therefore, to understand the language of the mantra, nor is there any need for mental speculation or any intellectual adjustment for chanting this maha-mantra. It springs automatically from the spiritual platform, and as such, anyone can take part in the chanting without any previous qualification, and dance in ecstasy. We have seen this practically.
Even a child can take part in the chanting, or even a dog can take part in it. Of course, for one who is too entangled in material life, it takes a little more time to come to the standard point, but even such a materially engrossed man is raised to the spiritual platform very quickly. When the mantra is chanted by a pure devotee of the Lord in love, it has the greatest efficacy on the hearers, and as such, this chanting should be heard from the lips of a pure devotee of the Lord, so that immediate effects can be achieved.

The word Hara is the form of addressing the energy of the Lord, and the words Krsna and Rama are forms of addressing the Lord Himself. Both Krsna and Rama mean "the supreme pleasure," and Hara is the supreme pleasure energy of the Lord, changed to Hare in the vocative. The supreme pleasure energy of the Lord helps us to reach the Lord. The material energy, called maya, is also one of the multienergies of the Lord. And we, the living entities, are also the energy—marginal energy—of the Lord. The living entities are described as superior to material energy. When the superior energy is in contact with the inferior energy, an incompatible situation arises; but when the superior marginal energy is in contact with the superior energy, called Hara, the living entity is established in his happy, normal condition.

These three words, namely Hare, Krsna, and Rama, are the transcendental seeds of the maha-mantra. The chanting is a spiritual call for the Lord and His internal energy, Hara, to give protection to the conditioned soul. This chanting is exactly like the genuine cry of a child for its mother. Mother Hara helps the meditator achieve the grace of the supreme father, Hari, or Krsna, and the Lord reveals Himself to the devotee who chants this mantra sincerely. No other means of spiritual realization, therefore, is as effective in this age as chanting the maha-mantra: Hare Krsna, Hare Krsna, Krsna Krsna, Hare Hare/ Hare Rama, Hare Rama, Rama Rama, Hare Hare.

This Mantra can be repeated and practiced by chanting it on beads, between ring-finger and thumb holding one bead at a time and consciously repeating Hare Krsna Hare Krsna Krsna Krsna Hare Hare Hare Rama Hare Rama Rama Rama Hare Hare.

This affirmation can be translated as follows:

'O divine energy,
Supplier of everything,
Source of Joy and Happiness.'

'O dear friend,
How can I serve you?'
'Most wonderful beloved, how can I make you happy?'

'Wonderful life, how can I live fully?'

'Please dear Friend, shine your smile.'

All these affirmations use a question, inquiry and bid to form a desire to know and to address. Affirmations are only fully potent when addressing a personality with a certain mood of honest relation.

There are five great types of reference or relationship, namely neutral, servitorship, friendly, parental and conjugal. All these have one thing in common: It is always a relation from person to person, from personality to personality.

No toaster or car should be praised or asked for, without including a personality. This aspect makes everything a personal trait, like:

'Please let this kitchen be clean! For
My friend, parent, children or spouse.'

See, there is always personality involved, therefore, to activate an affirmation one should address a person directly.
The Maha-Mantra is the address to the Original Personality and Supreme Personality.

Be aware of the mood you are sitting in, be present and prepare the affirmations carefully. Light a candle and maybe erect an altar that helps to focus the intention unto the desired outcome, for example:

A beautiful altar is filled with precious gems for protection and images of loved-ones. One can now affirm;

May all beings be protected and safe,
May my family be healthy and happy,
May I be healthy and happy.

I can take care of myself and of my family,
I can help the world by being myself, in goodness.
I trust a better world to be, in happiness and unity.

I am safe and sound, You are safe and sound, We are safe and sound. Let us breathe and unite in peace. Let us give thanks and gratitude to every breath.

May we all be aware that life is a miracle,
May you see the beauty within,
And may I connect to the highest Truth.

The focus is the most dominant guardian for any endeavour. Therefore, to remain focused and balance one needs a proper space and community. The right, meditative space will allow miracles to happen; as a seeing goes:

One can only grow as great as ones surrounding.

For example, no Giant Mammoth tree can grow in the dense jungle, only in a grove where there is proper space and circumstance, by time, the tree can unfold as a giant.

Universal Affirmation

Sit peacefully, relaxed and in a meditative space of tranquillity. Be prepared for sound, so find a comfortable seat or lay down flat. In both ways, when meditating face North and open the palms to the sky.

This hand gesture means 'openness', or
'ready to receive'.

Now use breath to calm down the mind and continue with equal breathing for a few deep moments. Let the inhale and exhale be equal and focus on the heart.
Notice the constant stream of air flowing along the nose tip, in and out it goes. Very equally and rhythmically. Body, spine, emotions and mind are in alignment and balance.

Feel the ground, either on the buttocks or with the whole body. Be aware of the whole body as a unit. This wholeness starts within the heart. Focus here and breathe equally, with an equanimous mind.

Whatever thoughts arise, be aware and let them pass. Don't worry, like ebb and flood, thoughts arise and fade naturally. Just observe this phenomenon and keep balance.

Balance is everything. In a Space, to create balance, one can utter the syllable AUM. This word (ॐ) or Omkara is the whole manifestation of the All-attractive Supreme Personality.

When we utter this sound, the whole body vibrates in a natural frequency. Simultaneously, it is a greeting to address the Supreme Reservoir of all things and worlds.

This divine sound is very simple, yet ultimately profound. One can hear this resonance everywhere in nature, for example in the rivers or even within the breath. Be aware of the sound of the breath and just listen for some equal breaths.

Breathe, equally in and equally out again. Be aware of the sound and let it sink into the heart space.

Here is the centre of Attraction and one can witness how the whole body is maintained from here. Let the sound of the breath evenly sink into the belly and to the feet.

Be aware of the sensations and remain in balance.

Now, one can utter the sound. The mouth is fully open to start uttering the Aaaahh, as long as possible. This sound A vibrates within the abdomen or more specifically within the area of the navel. This is the sound of creation.
Now, you can utter the sound U, nice and long. Keep it, maintain and feel it. This sound vibrates within the heart space, straight up the spine, and it is the manifestation of Unity and connection.
Now, you can utter the sound Mmm. The mouth is completely closed and it vibrates in the area of the throat. Keep it inside and let it sound, even up to the crown of your head. The whole jaw, skull, neck and shoulders are addressed with this sound of purity.
So, A-U-M are three individual sounds, in a connected flow of sound. This is pure, creative energy which addresses the Supreme reservoir of all Attraction.

Sound and Tone: AaaaUuuuMmm. Feel it, vibrate with it and let it free naturally.

Practice makes perfect. Repeat and rehearse. This sound is to create space and purify existence. It addresses also the lake of consciousness just on the feet of the Supreme Attractor whose eyes are like the sun and moon.

So let's speak to the heart's content, addressing the Supreme Attractor in person, one can utter this sacred sound which acts as a spiritual key for tuning in and saying Hello.

Of course, the Supreme Personality is always very nice to devotees who are thus addressing his abode and Reservoir of all pleasure:

'Om (A-U-M), O highest person, please accept my humble request, I am here to learn how to purely meditate...

May this meditation lead to Your Reservoir of abundance, pleasantness and attraction.'

Thus, the highest person who sits within our hearts knows what is our desire and can listen.

When, in meditation, one shall know what to attract: Let's say, ,One wants to attract... a pure and healthy life', or ',...a good way to learn for my exam. 'one can easily say it. From the heart, everything is accepted. Just be humble and utter your wishes internally, externally, or write it down.

We shall for now envision internally, but we will come back to external, and contemplative methods like meditation.

Just imagine why you came here. What is the purpose of your visit?

Like a messenger comes to the King and reports news or proposes an inquiry, one can be inquisitive and ask for anything. The Supreme Reservoir in person understands and is always open to granting a conversation or even permission.

Good things, prescribed in scriptures, like purity or the search for the absolute Truth are always welcome.

This Truth is essentially within everyone's heart and thus one carries it around everywhere.

Meditation means also internal contemplation. Therefore, help yourself with enough time and space. Five-minute meditations fill a gap or can be integrated before a meal, proper sit, breathe and meditate. Meditation can thus make every life circumstance a conscious effort for attraction and well-being. Meditation creates space, like with a Mantra (Om), and within this space, one can attract anything. Be patient and listen. Enough space for meditation is necessary to feel purity and abundance holistically.

Light Affirmation

There is a Mantra, an affirmation, on how to still the mind, and create good vibrations. It goes like this:

I am the Light of the World,
I am the Light of the World,
I am, I am, I am the Light of the World.

You are the Light of the world,
You are the Light of the World,
You are, You are, You are the Light of the World.

We are the Light of the World,
We are the Light of the World,
We are, We are, We are the Light of the World.

Light is life. Light is love.
Light is everything around.

With every light, one can blink and address the eyes, the receivers of light.

Blink and let the eyes shine. Smile and give thanks for the light.

With steady practice of this Mantra, one can still the mind and attract light in dark times.
Light can be interchanged with everything that makes life liveable, like:

I am the Love of the World,
You are the Love of the World,
We are the Love of the World.

I am the Peace of the World,
You are the Peace of the World,
We are the Peace of the World.

I am the Unity of the World,
You are the Unity of the World,
We are the Unity of the World.

Or speak an affirmation of goodness, purity and blessing.

I am attracting Goodness now and forever,
You are attracting Goodness within time,
We are attracting Goodness evermore.

Let purity bring Me closer to myself,
Let purity bring Us closer together,
Let purity bring Them closer to themselves

May all beings be blessed,
May the world, time and circumstance be blessed.

Affirmation work effectively through devotion and repetition, therefore repeat these phrases in perfect alignment. Feel the purpose and need for the affirmation knowing that words attract, whatever we say.

In regards to sacred Mantras like AUM and Affirmation, it is most common to create a mood of prayer including honesty and compassion.

Thank you for this light, thank you to shine bright
Thanks for all the love from the sky above.

Thankfulness, Truth and Compassionate Love.

Sitting upright and align to sky and earth, being grounded and free to speak is the basis of every good meditation.

To create a meditative place one can speak the following formulas, to purify a meditation room:

May this space be clean and free of envy, anger and other things,
May this place serve for meditation and affirmation.
May I find a comfortable seat.

To speak honestly means also to speak in full understanding of the purpose. Why Am I here? To meditate, ok. Let the room know, light a candle or incense and find your own space of tranquillity.

Create an oasis of abundance within the heart, as well as within the living space. Practically, every space can be transformed into a meditative space.

Everybody is a temple and everyone is living in their temple.

One who knows about the sanctity of a space can still the lake of consciousness easily. Thus, wishes and desires are reflected perfectly and the ground can be visible.

From the ground sometimes unconscious or stored attractions are coming to the surface. Like a habit, a thought pattern, or a simple word. These can be fetched, transformed and used with the matter of the breath and consciousness. Everything in life has a reason, a ground to exist.

It is a balance about moving and being, speaking and receiving. Prepare a well-balanced place, safely and protected, in a sacred setting of peace and tranquility. This may be the soil for good growth.

Give thanks to the heart, the spiritual heart where sweet Balance resides. This focus can be a gaze that is shifted within, towards the heart, or easier to the middle of the face, on the nose-tip. A candle light helps to focus this attention.

See a nice candle flickering on this altar and continue meditating, in silence, to cleanse the space.
Affirm safety and protection, trust and happiness.

'With every word I affirm that this space is sacred and spiritual, safe and peaceful.
May peace and protection surround this place for the whole while.
May I trust in the higher good for all.'

Affirm in mind, word or even writing.

'I am the Light of the World,

I am the Light of the World,
I am, I am, I am the Light of the World.'

'You are the Light of the World.
You are the Light of the World,
You are, you are, you are the Light of World.'

'We are the Light of the World.
We are the Light of the World,
We are, we are, we are the Light of the World.'

Put your palms on your heart and breathe equally. Relax and let the affirmation sink in.
Be aware of the subtle vibration of sound and harmony within the heart. Feel the pulse and notice that light and lightness is filling your heart.

Light is essential, so is the identification with a certain aspect of life. Life is light, therefore it resounds everywhere. Light is the great base of all life and connector of all living beings.

Appreciate the heart, the light and personality. Personality expresses itself through (per) sound (sonar). Personality is the light within every movement, thought and character. It is the essence of all life. Life itself has character and it is light, full of wisdom, eternal and blissful.

Life is intelligent and we can make life a good friend, as we speak nice words and craft pleasant thoughts. For every circumstance there are affirmations, for example when a loved-one is not well, or when trust is lacking, or when we ask for forgiveness, or before a supper.

With patience and understanding one can turn life into a prayerful affirmation of goodness and grace.
A life in harmony is thus attainable through sacred sound vibration and affirmation.

<u>Waking up with affirmations:</u>

May this day be fulfilled with light and joy,
 May I give thanks to nature, the earth and sky,
to family and friends, and all living beings.
May all beings be light-hearted and happy, joyful at peace.
I find success and ease within every breeze.
May the life air help me to relief.
I breathe happiness and joy.

To confirm your inner Truth, wake up with these prayers:

I affirm and encourage others, as I do myself.
I alone hold the truth of who I am.

Bring affirmations into daily life and see how a mindset can make a good morning.

Before dressing you can speak following affirmations:

I am beautiful and I can see the beauty in others. My heart is full of grace and pleasure.
I shall attract goodness with who I am. I am who I am.

I am wearing a mindset of peace and unity, I am wearing this for my beloved friends, family, workmates or surrounding. I just want to be beautiful. May all I do and wear be a sign of inner trust and truth.

Dresses make people, a saying goes, but it is really the mindset and focus that can attract people and goodness. A dress does make a difference, subtle, but noticeable it is the consciousness behind all we do and focus how we act. Clean and natural clothing are an expression of ones mood, therefore be aware of how you dress your inner state of consciousness. Basically, clothing means protection. Protection from the cold, the heat, the sun, or the glances of others. Keep in mind, that affirmations are a simply wonderful way of protection and shelter.

Affirmations during midday or before lunch:
May all living beings be equally happy and in balance.
May all beings be safe and protected, happy and content.
I let go of all distress and fear, knowing to be safe.
This space is a sacred space of transformation.
In gratitude I bow to the higher personality within.

During the day, the higher personality is guiding us, and if one is attentive and listens, then grace and blessings come with inquiry.

As we ask, so we receive.
Here, honesty is most valuable.

Please, may I have shelter from lower conditions and stressful circumstances.

May I receive the shelter of your grace and be protected by calamities.

May all beings be kind and friendly.

May I serve for the highest of human.

Is there a higher truth?
I am just to see. Where shall I look?
What is the purpose of my life or this sitauation?

Some might call it the fourth and fifth dimension within the living entity. However, affirmations work through polarity and attraction. It is like a play of call and response. When having a sacred sound vibration or Mantra, like the Maha-Mantra Hare Krsna Hare Krsna Krsna Krsna Hare Hare Hare Rama Hare Rama Rama Rama Hare Hare then this can be sung in a certain way. Usually this affirmation in musical form is called kirtan or chanting of the holy name. There is a slight mystery and wonder within this process, therefore it is recommend to experience it.

When one is calling Hare Hare! Or Divine Light! Then, within the pause, there is an echo or answer. Something within reciprocates and gives resolution to what has been said or called out for.

Therefore, listening is so important. Listen to your inner voice and be aware of slight changes. Breathe in-between and notice differences and alterations.

Affirmations to increase life satisfaction

This meditation takes the form of a mantra. You can repeat the affirmations silently inside your mind or out loud if you prefer. Allow yourself to really feel the words and let them resonate.

Repeat each fresh phrase like a Kirtan, call and response.

I am satisfied with all there is,
Nothing more, nothing less,
Balance in equanimity,
Feel Peace and Harmony.
I am satisfied with you,
Content and true,
Here and Now,
I take a bow
Silence in my mind,
Love in my heart,
We are all a part
Of a wonder world,
From the breath,
From east to the west,
I Live to try the best.
I affirm to be content
Here and Now,
With All there is
On the way to bliss,
I bow, Balance is now
Silence in my mind,
Love in my heart,
We are all a part,

Of this moment world,
A Moment to Moment,
Breathe and feel,
Peace, Love and Unity
I affirm Harmony
Within all there is,
I am bliss,
I am Balance,
I am equanimity,
Peace, love and unity.
I meditate upon the Wholeness,
Balance for everyone,
Peace for everyone,
Love for everyone,
Unity for everyone,
Harmony for everyone,
Bliss for everyone
I meditate upon the Highest Absolute,
May you be merciful with Us,
May we serve for the highest good of all,
May we All live in Peace and Harmony.
Love and Unity,
Here and Now,
I bow.

This concludes positive Affirmations.

Guided Meditations for Panic attacks

Wherever one is, the breath is with you. It is the medicine for the soul to be consciously breathing. This medicine everyone always lives with. We have just forgotten, that the breath is with us, and likewise stilling any panic or distress. Sudden help needed? Just breathe, 21, 22, 23... be aware of the breath. Notice the heart, the feet and belly. Touch can also bring us back. Touch the flap of the ear and notice the soft fingertips. Be aware of Balance always through the matter of the breath and remember, breathe, and never forget.

Remember one is alive, with the breath, the life-long friend, and like music, the breath gives one constant inspiration and background. Humans have mistakes and failures, no problem, it is how one handles them. The primer is to always stay in balance. How? Conscious breathing is the way. Always equal, and with an equanimous mind. Focus the nose-tip and let the eyes be half closed and half open. Breathe consciously, and notice that the mechanism of the breath is natural.

By own effort, one can breathe, by own effort one can react and by own effort one can remain in tranquil and peaceful balance. There is no worry, just keep breathing and remembering to always be aware of that. Conscious means to see it happen, presently, and to listen. So now, listen to the breath and be aware of how it sounds. Sometimes like an ocean, sometimes like the wind. The life air streams into the nostrils, and to the lungs around the heart. How does this sound like?

Be aware and just continue on breathing, notice the light stream of air on the nose tip touching the nostrils and entering into the head. Keep the eyes within and notice the sensation. Sometimes there is cold or warmth, or tickling, throbbing or vibrating. Just keep on breathing and remain equal.

Be aware of the breath in balance, inhale and exhale equally streaming in and out, same length, same intensity. This is balanced breath. Whatever thought arises, just keep on breathing. Remember to be noticing the breath and come to the senses and the mind, come to the heart and feel the heart beat. One is Alive. How grateful one can be.

Panic, like any other disturbance of the mind has its root in anger. Anger arises from Lust and when the senses are too attached to something, then lust arises from attachment. The medicine for this process of being panic-free is detachment.

Detachment of the senses and mind can easily be practiced under the guidance of a teacher, but lets make it possible with a little meditation:

Find ease within the matter of the breath. Inhale equal. Inhale, one, two, three, four. Embrace. Exhale, one, two, three, four. Let the natural breath take over and sit comfortably in a sacred space. Let the meditation sink into the heart. Let the breathing flow to the sacred heart space and be aware of the slight and subtle sensations. Whatever arises, let it pass and focus on the nose tip, remaining with an equanimous mind, always in balance, whatever sensation arises, also fades. One stays equal with the breath. Anything can happen, but the sacred space within the heart hosts eternity, wisdom and bliss.

Within this meditation one can experience a safe shelter, where, when necessary, one can come back to. It is a sacred space of love and peace. Here unity resides, in person, and forever. Ones personality needs to be protected from any circumstance, therefore no panic, this place is always with one, within the heart. Here eternity, wisdom and bliss reside, also. It is an everlasting abode of consciousness.

Within this consciousness one is aware of the free space within meditation. As the breathing comes and goes, one finds shelter within the realm of bliss, happy consciousness. It is a castle of sacred rose quartz, built in the heavenly kingdom of ones heart. This place is surrounded with an effulgence glow of rose, purple and light blue. The heavenly kingdom is protected by many heavenly guards and warriors who are all trustful in the mission to maintain peace. Like one is maintaining the body for a life, similarly, these guardians are sheltering the eternal kingdom of peace and love with humility and weapons of light and harmony.

One is now invited to come along, to be a temporary guest within the Heart community of consciousness. This castle has doors and windows framed with golden ornaments. Huge, heavy doors open and a protective Angel shines a smile and waves for a greeting. Genuine and humble, dressed in white, flowing robes, the Protective Angel glances over ones face and whatever sensation now arises, let it sink in and pass. Breathe equally and feel invited to come into this sacred place in full protection and peace.

The door step is a mosaic of planets like earth, moon and sun, and the first sight falls upon a shelf of sacred scriptures. The entrance is a library! All the literature imagine-able is present in this endless space of wisdom. One can have a stroll along the long lines of the shelves and maybe one finds a little inspiration to read. Take it easy, this place is safe and equipped with endless time. The planets are guarding this room with personal affirmations: The Sunshine protects one from disease, the moon is there for ones heart and mind, the Venus for ones relationships and emotions, Mars for ones chivalry, Jupiter for ones majesty, Saturn for ones learning and listening, Neptune for ones compassion, Pluto for ones spiritual intuition and earth for ones humility.
Humble as one can be, glad and satisfied, grateful and appreciative, having earth means to be presently thankful and aware, all is in care. Just breathe and be safe within this heavenly castle of rose quartz, within the library of dreams.

One can move on into to the dinner hall where endless dishes are provided by heavenly cooks and servants all dressed in beautiful white robes with garlands around their necks. Golden plates are carried around and full bowls of silver are served to the guests who are relishing the tasty delicacies. One can see kings, ministers, priests, men, children, women, even beggars and monks, travelers, explorers, scientists, sportsmen and hospital clowns. All are feasting on the same table and there are plenty of seats free for one to be seated.

Sit comfortable and breathe equally, remain aware and ask yourself, what kind of relieve you like from a stressed day full of panic, anger, sorrow, grief and mistrust, what would give relief? Maybe some ice-cream with bananas and berries? Or the speciality of the castle? A full buffet with endless choices of all you can eat? Why not contemplate about it, take it easy and just envision a course of freshly prepared dishes coming your way on golden plates, right here, in front of you, a thirty dish menu unfolds and waits for ones enthusiasm.

Enthusiastically, a cabaret of showmen entertains the assembled guests with a show of many varieties like magic tricks, stand-up comedy, stories and a unique character. This show is full of laughter and absurdity, humorous and funny, slightly interesting but even so delicious. The food is almost finished, when a musical orchestra comes out to perform classical pieces for dance. The music is very beautiful and soothing, the feet are tapping and one can embrace the slight beat. The rhythm changes and everyone is invited to dance. A full party unfolds into a profound, yet peaceful dance party, swinging from left to right, turning and setting every step at the exact perfect place. A heavenly dance unfolds.

Like a blossom flower unfolds within nature through the sun shining light towards the bud, a living being can bloom through a light mood of unity. In this Assembly of the rose quartz castle one can also witness a sacred ceremony called an Arati, a light ceremony. Within the next space, there is a temple situated, very brightly lit, and decorated with silver and gold, flowers and sacred plants, artifacts and sacred scriptures, where in the very front is a great altar covered with a curtain. When the curtain opens one calls this Darshan, or sacred sight, a spiritual experience where one can actually witness the heavenly realms within. The altar is also made of rose quartz, and down one, two steps comes a priest, bare feet, dressed in saffron silks. He has a big, hand-sized conch shell within his hands and puts it to his mouth to blow a very deep, loud and long sound, combining all the oceans and rivers. So loud, everyone can hear it. A bell rings nicely, and the curtain opens to present the deities of the Supreme Lord, the owner of the rose quartz castle and the whole universe. Priests are fanning the Supreme Personality with great awe and reverence.

The Supreme Personality has bare feet seated on a cushion, and the whole body is dressed in purple, dark rose, red and blue silks and finest garments. Holding a book in the one hand, and in the other hand a flute. The smile with the sweetness eternally fulfills all hearts and brings joy to the guests and visitors. There is a wonderful crown on the head, a halo of light surrounds the Personality.

Remaining still and peaceful, the Perosnality is much obliged by the visitors and greets them friendly, holding up the flute and inquiring if one has danced enough. Maybe it is time to read from the sacred scriptures?
The guests are eager to listen.

Now, listen to the breath and be aware of any subtle sensation. Be steady and in full awareness of the heart, mind and imagination. Breathe, and relax. There is a personality within every heart that is full of transcendental joy and happiness, always safe and in trust, mystical and inconceivable, yet safely placed on a throne within the castle of consciousness. Safely protected by guardians of peace and Angels of Protection, well fed and entertained.

Darshan is said to be the means to purify ones eyes and heart from the contamination of material existence. There is life and death, there is distress and happiness, coming and going, uniting and separating, rising and passing away. Like the breath teaches us to be real, one can see real Darshan in ancient temples all over the world. It is as real, as the spiritual world made of touch stone, a precious stone that takes on any form and character. The Personality is the Supreme Lord of all spiritual worlds and hearts. Within everyone this Personality resides and connects.

All are united through this Personality. Union, thus, is the one simple truth that gives us all equality within this life. Whenever there is doubt, separation, or fear, one can remember this safe space of consciousness. Instantly one can be here, within this castle of consciousness. Here, everything is blissful and eternal.
Just breathe and be aware of the subtle link between breathing, mind, body and reality. Notice the legs, feet, and tippy toes. Relax. Notice the belly, solar plexus, chest and upper chest. Relax. Be aware of the heart beat, notice it and relax. Relax the arms, elbows, wrists, palms, fingers and fingertips. Relax the shoulders, neck and jaw. Relax the head and crown. The whole body is relaxed. Prepare for a conscious, blissful relaxation.

With every breath, there is peace streaming into the body, with the matter of the breath. There is tranquility, peace and serenity. Let the anger, panic, fear and doubt go with every breath and let the body sink into relaxation. Notice and be aware of how the mind is still active and present. Notice the nose tip and be aware of the consciousness.

Like the heaven, the matter of sky, is very clear and subtle, pervading all elements, including water, fire and earth, it holds the powerful wind, within its boundaries. The air is the great purifier of all purifiers and it is the connecting link between, body, mind and consciousness. When the consciousness is clear, one can see through it, like one can see the stars on a beautiful night sky. When the mindful clouds arise, the sight is dimmed.

Be aware of the beautiful soothing moonshine, even now. Notice it, and relax. Both, in and exhale are like sun and moon, always rising, and fading. Essentially, both are in a dance with one another.

Similarly, this interplay is like a dance of lover and beloved. Inhale and exhale behave like two lovers in a dance, constantly inviting each other and separating. The matter of breathing symbolizes the invitation of the lover to dance. When the inhale takes place, there is union, and for a moment, everything is within harmony. A small moment of unity resolves and the exhale ignites the separation, one lets go of the matter of breath and the dancing lovers symbolically part. A small moment passes within this separation and the whole dance begins again.

The duality of sensations are also described further:

'The non permanent appearance of happiness and distress, and their disappearance in due course, are like the appearance and disappearance of winter and summer seasons. They arise from sense perception, and one must learn to tolerate them without being disturbed.'

(Bhagavād-Gita, 2.14)

When the mind and senses are detached from temporary material longings, then the flower of the soul can blossom.

The Supreme Personality within the conscious castle knows very well how to eliminate all panic, by spiritual means.

Meditation and detachment are the means, but truly one can only be free of all material suffering, when fully conscious of the divine nature of life.

Thus, meditation helps one, in the moment, counting simply as 21, 22, 23 or even diving deeper into the root cause of all panics, and anxiety. All these root in the material endeavour of temporary illusion, or Maya. This illusion is difficult to overcome, yet one can meditate upon the Supreme Reservoir of all Balance and Peace and thus attain peace. From this spiritual peace happiness can unfold and give plenty of wisdom and blessings to all.

No panic, all the wisdom and help is within the heart, in the eternal library and within the consciousness of oneself. This meditation is based on scriptural evidence and thousands of years of application. Just trust in the process of meditation and one may attain a blissful state of being.

Meditating with Supreme Abundance

From the natural periphery, we start our meditative journey to the personal nature.

This nature is essentially eternal and full of abundance.

This abundance comes in energy and with quality. It has character as well as form and personality.

Be aware of this present situation and breathe. Gently in and out again, equal and aware, every breath is likewise streaming into the nose, and out again. Loosen the muscles on the shoulders, and neck, and open up the chest with a straight posture.

The life air is flowing into the nostrils and reaching the heart. Here, all attraction happens.

The heart is the spiritual abode of personality and bliss, everlasting wisdom and eternity.

Be aware of the breath touching the heart and notice it streaming out again. This process of conscious breathing keeps the focus on the subject matter.

The subject of personality is connected to a sense of self, or ego, which naturally expresses a desire. One is just aware of this thought, whatever it may be.

This is the matter of the mind, and the senses, knowing very well that there is coming and going of the breath.

Notice the duality of in-and-out of the breathing. Are both equal?
Inhale one... two... three... four, exhale one... two... three... four. Pause for a moment. Repeat. Inhale one... two... three... four, exhale one... two... three... four.

Imagine sitting on a still lake of consciousness. The moon is shining in full and the light is reflected very authentically on the lake. This still lake receives the light of the moon very nicely, and hence the lake is still, the light can shine through the surface onto the ground of the lake.

The light is both reflected by the still lake of consciousness and touched deeply to the ground of the unconscious. Both are reached and pervaded by crystal clear moonlight.

Pure Sunshine Meditation

Just sit, together with the Supreme Person who is very beautiful and renounced on the lake of consciousness. It is almost sunrise, and the sky is glowing very beautifully. See the stars and planets on the firmament, these are like all the persons, forefathers, masters, saints and heavenly beings in innumerable numbers. Knowing the sun comes up, the Supreme reservoir of light unfolds.

The rays of this sunlight spread internally and externally, from within the solar-plexus translucent light is emanating around the heart, shoulders, arms, hands, hips, legs, feet and head. The bliss and energy of the sunshine spreads around the whole being and warmth is present.

The horizon now gives a sense of smile. Golden and brilliant, the effulgence of the sun purifies all the senses and equips one with happiness and comfort.

Consciously breathe and equally feel the breath. Rhythmically in and out again. Very equal, and with an equanimous mind. The light of the sunshine makes one smile, and happiness and joy are attracted, like flowers of a tree blossom when touching the sunlight.
Smile, be happy and content. All the joy, happiness and love is surrounding you.

Meditation for Depression

<u>Happiness Meditation</u>

Be aware of the breathing. Moment to Moment one can notice how the breathing is equally streaming in and out. The breath is very subtle yet profound, streaming into the nostrils and flowing to the heart. From here the whole life air is distributed all over the body. The body is charged with life energy and happiness.

Happiness can come in many ways, but the easiest is light. Light is always present and can be transformed into anything one likes to attract. The human body is like a magnet with two poles, and like light, it has a dual character. When there is balance in the body through meditation. Happiness can ignite a fire of freedom and bliss.

So, breathe equally and mindfully. The mind is sometimes compared to a flickering lamp, but one who is steady in meditation can easily still the flickering of the lamp. This is the purpose of meditation.

See this lamp, or candle within your vision and know that from one candle one can ignite many more candles, easily this can be done from a simple hand.

Sit equally and in a comfortable position. Put one hand on the area of the navel and breathe equally. Feel, how the belly rises and sinks with every breath. With inhalation, the belly rises, and with exhalation, the belly sinks to normal.

Just be aware of the balance between inhalation and exhalation. Let it be the basis for a steady and happy meditation.

An endless source of happiness is found within the heart, therefore, let's focus on the heart and its beat. This beat is the rhythm of one's life. Now, put one hand onto the chest and feel the heartbeat.

Be aware and notice its character, what does the heart say? What is within the heart's desire? Is the rhythm equal and in harmony?

Just notice the beats and sit straight. Now, use your hand to move in a clockwise circle around the chest area and belly. Let it be a flowing movement, connecting both heart and belly.

Breathe, and smile.

Now, use the hands to swipe the other parts of the body. Just swipe. Eventually, one can do this sweeping with the awareness, cleansing the whole body, energy and mind.

Now, come back to the heart and happiness. Smile, again. Breathe equally in and out. Let the smile sink into the heart and remember a moment of happiness within your life. Maybe just very recently, what did make you considerably happy?

Let it be a simple thing, like a smile, and continue seeing this memory to be present and within the heart. Let the memory pass, and breathe equally.

Be aware of your whole body. Now, remember a person that makes you especially happy. See this person in form and character, with full heart and within the inner vision. Be aware of the moment with the person, right here within the heart. Breathe and let it sink into the garden of the heart. Welcome to the lake of consciousness, where everybody is fully in balance, peace and happiness.

The Supreme Abundance greets also from this place of the heart. Breathe equally and come to ease. Sweet birds are flying around the sacred trees, making the atmosphere very wonderful and serene. Can you see the lake of consciousness? Is it still? Are you aware of the little sensations that are going on, maybe warmth or cold, tickling, throbbing, vibrating. Just focus on the heart and the garden of a happy heart.

All together with the Supreme Abundance who sits very comfortably on a cushioned throne overlooking the lake of consciousness, garlanded and scented very nicely, Supreme Abundance is smiling and inviting to have a comfortable position to see the sunset.

Happiness can be so simple, like watching a sunset together. The lake of consciousness is very nicely reflecting the effulgent rays of the sun, turning the whole atmosphere into a joyful place. As the golden globe enchants and enlights everything with a tranquil glow of happiness one can witness the sweet songs of the birds. A natural symphony creates balance within the system and here, in this heartful land, there is no lack of happiness.

One can be grateful and appreciative to be here, and now. Breathing equally in and out, in respect to nature and heaven. One can give thanks to the light, especially of the sun who provides blissful light to everyone.

By folding the hands together, and holding the palms on the chest, and in front of the heart one can speak the following affirmations:

Thanks Giving to the Light,
May all beings be happy,
Shine bright into the night,
May all beings be happy.

Even in the darkness,
There is happiness,
Love and Lightness,
always in bliss.

In every heart, and every breath.
In and out, equally breathe and relax.
Let the sunlight give healing and happy light to the core and notice that even the sunshine shines from within. A simple smile makes a perfect sun,
glowing and igniting the spark of happiness in everyone.

Now one can affirm happiness and prosperity in one's life:

May I attract happiness and love,
May all beings be happy and loved.
May love and happiness surround all.

Happiness shall fill my life,
My life and every life.
Happiness shall speak to me,
May all beings happy and free.

May prosperity be present,
May I see health and happiness.
Abundance for the world and I.
May all beings be happy and free.

Sit in a comfortable position and open the palms to the sky. Just receive. Be content and satisfied, happily awaiting the bliss.

It is already there, you see? Breathe and be happy.
Within endless energy of heart and soul, one can fetch the happiest of all: Life. From life comes love and from love comes life. Life is already filled with happiness, one just needs to be open, trusting and receptive.

Trust in your ability to trust and be patient, breath by breath a conscious relationship with the abundant heart takes place. This is the best way. Breathing equally, and remaining in balance. In and out, rhythmically, with great attention to the sensations. From the nose-tip to the heart, and from the heart to the belly. Happiness has taste and a wonderful feeling. Be aware of the emotional sensations and continue, giving attention to the heartbeat.

Envision a brilliant light pervading the matter of the body, flowing from the heart like a pure river of consciousness into the energy channels of the body. From the belly, the whole body is nurtured, likewise with energy. Therefore be aware of the light around the abdomen and let the awareness spread around the hips, legs, knees, ankles and feet. Let the light of awareness rise into the upper body parts again, streaming from the feet to the ankles, knees, thighs and lower body, to the upper body, chest, back, shoulders, arms and hands. Let the light of awareness now find the head. The neck, shoulders, jaw, chin and ears are all surrounded by beautiful, conscious light. Around the eyes, and on the crown of the head the light finds expression and blossoms into a sweet golden lotus flower.

See every petal of the lotus flower as a unique and magnificent creation. See it shining, embrace it and be aware that the lotus flower cannot be polluted, or contaminated. It has a protective layer that holds away all impurities. Embrace this pure golden lotus flower, and let it grow in the lake of consciousness.
Offer this lotus flower to the Supreme Abundance and hold the beauty and golden splendour of the sun within the heart. Breathe, equally in and out. Be aware of the sensations around the heart, body and mind.

Rest in this position and consciously focus on the nose-tip. By breathing in, one can connect a thought to the breath. By breathing out, one can let go of a thought. Be aware, and inhale with the thought of pure light. Exhale with the thought of letting go.
Inhale with the thought of golden happiness, exhale with the thought of letting go. Inhale with the thought of protection and peace, exhale and let go of fear, anxiety and pain.

With every breath, there is an exchange of energy and transformation happening. One can transform the subtle energy of the breath into life force, and thus attracting the life one desires. Through the permission of the Supreme Personality, one can receive all the protection, abundance and prosperity, health, happiness and freedom.

Supreme Balance, please help one to release stagnating energy that needs to be relieved. Sublime Light, may I have your guidance and light to dissolve the unwanted energies. Let there be Breath.
We tune into he Life Energy Force by opening our hands and asking for guidance. Simply ask.
Stress is mostly affecting our gut, inner organs, and nervous system, but can be relieved through the navel. Same with deep depression. It can be resolved as we come back to our mothers' life-giving channel. Place one hand for Life Force energy onto the navel, and another hand slightly higher from the chest, between the heart and throat chakra, to release and resolve the emotions that do not serve anymore. Imagine a wonderful healing flow streaming from the belly button to the heart center, from the heart to the throat, and slightly open your jaw, unclench and relax it. Let the energy flow for a good few minutes and wait so you feel the breathing. Breathing into the belly, breathing equally in and out, focus on the breath and feel the energy flow. Release the hands and give yourself a nice and soothing head and jaw massage. Release all tension and listen to soothing music.

Nurture and Compassion

Healing relationships and connections may be one of the higher goals in life. However, by healing ourselves, we heal others. By strengthening the connection to ourselves, our bodies, emotions and thoughts, we empower the connection to all around us. To nurture compassion and love put both of your hands onto the chest and you may be able to form a triangle with your fingers. Put this triangle on your chest and let it face in one direction. Feel and Embrace energy. Ask Supreme Balance for Guidance and Help, Receive and Trust. Close your eyes and breathe naturally.

A few minutes later, embrace change and alter the direction of the triangle to see the change. Breathe equally in and out. Relax and concentrate within the Heart space. Feel and energize your chest with a few deep breaths. Sink into meditation or play music.

Self-esteem

Feeling a lower sense of self can sometimes be depressing or even a way to imbalance, however, it is all just the Solar energy stagnating or without a proper balance. Our hands help to focus and channel energy. Any kind of energy can be transmitted, but Breath is the universal Life force which includes all energies. It heals and responds, intelligently finding the way.
Ask the Supreme Light to heal, ask kindly to withdraw and receive energy from the source.
Breathe through, equally in and out, feel and receive Life force energy. Be aware of the breath and focus on the entrance of the nostrils. Put your hand slightly below the chest and above the belly into the sternum. The solar plexus resides within the body and takes care of the strength and power, acting as a channel between belly and brain. Put the other hand on the forehead or on the side of the head, close to the jaw and ear area. Energy shall flow between the brain, the third eye chakra, and solar plexus. Hold the position and breathe accordingly. Harmonize the breathing, equally in and out. Feel the energy rising, flowing along the spine. Any sensation may arise with it, warmth, tingling, vibrating, but one shall keep breathing naturally and normal. Remain and Relax, open the hands facing upwards to the sky and close the eyes for a few minutes. Feel and breathe.

Gratitude for Good

We make a journey to our inner most feeling of gratitude, for us and for all.
:
We find a comfortable seat and give our attention to Mother Earth and the Ground. Feel the buttocks, feel the whole body being steady and well nurtured. The roots, are spreading widely into the floor and one feels the main column, the spine in balance. Now let the body be an endless place of discovery. The breath is the vehicle for your journey. We are looking for a place of endless gratitude and thanks.
Gratitude for this world, for all the living beings, for your family and friends.
Imagine with every single breath you start to shrink, smaller and smaller, you become so small, you are fitting into the nostril, even smaller you are so small you can fit into an oxygen particle, a very tiny piece of existence. Now you travel with the wind breathing in and there you are inside your nose. Inside the body, flowing in an endless stream of air down the throat and chest area into the lungs. You start to feel light, so small and tiny. With every breath you become lighter and lighter, so light, you can fit into the space between the lungs. There is an open cave, mysterious and beautifully decorated, rose colored and shimmering with light, you can now see through the skin to the heart. Feel the lightness and meet the Heartkeeper, a wonderful friend and friendly warrior.

Protecting your Heart, he knows who you are and bows in a gracious manner. You can now enter, the Heartkeeper says and we enter. The wide Palast-alike spaces allow a beautiful freedom to dance, sing and what you like it to be. Now we fill this Palast with gratitude and you will see how this palace is so great it holds place for everyone you invite. Breathe naturally and let thanks flow in. Let the breathing be natural and let gratitude flow in. Breathe out and let it anger and sorrow go.

Hold your palms together and join a prayer: I am thankful for my family,
I am thankful for my friends,
I am thankful for all the beings. x3

We come gently back to our guardian the Heartkeeper and give thanks from All our Heart. There is a Heartkeeper in everyone of Us and we now see all connections. All our Hearts are connected. We see a World wide connection of Heartkeepers.

We hold stillness for a while. We let our breathing become natural and flowing. Gently we put our hands over our face. We feel and sense the warmth of the palms. We blink and gently open our eyes. We massage our face and come to ease. Give yourself all the time, and return back to your normal size into this room. Let the palms open on your laps and give thanks to every one in the room.

I am thankful for U
I am thankful for U
 I am thankful for U

Meditation for Relaxation

Creating space to relax - Create space for relaxation with the meditation. Become aware of your thought processes and any tendencies that accompany your experience of relaxation.
Start meditating. Focus on your breath, equally flowing in and out. Equally in, equally out. Bring your attention to the sound of the breathing. Calming, soothing breath, flowing in and out. Let it flow naturally and listen in. By listening we open our gates to the soul. The connection of sound and space lets us relax. Creating space, listening, relax with every breath.
Let the breath come and go. See yourself easing into the simple process of breathing. Nothing more, nothing less. Just the breath. Just feel. Relax. Every thought arising, every thought passing. Remember the breath, coming and going, and again equally in and out. The thoughts may come and go - no need to do anything - just breathe.

Now, when you notice a thought coming, observe it. Just see it as it is and let it be. Like the breath, here to make us live. Feel the life with every breath. Feel the sensation of the chest rising with every inhale. Once you feel, just be aware of the sensation of the area around the heart. If you cannot feel, slightly hard breathe. Just a few times intensely breathing in, making space, being aware of the free flow. Let it flow naturally. According to the breathing thoughts may come and go. Just observe and be aware of any thought springing up. Let it flow, let it go, let it be. Feel free. With every breath, equally in, equally out. Sometimes the stream of thought is very strong, carrying us away, be attentive and aware. With a balanced mind we come home to our breathing. Naturally to the present moment with the power of the breath. Maintain balance and equanimity. Let the stream of thoughts just evenly be, relax and feel free. Feel free. Equanimity. Relax.

<u>A vision of relaxation</u>

Create a vision of relaxation in your mind. By focusing in on that mind picture, you can deepen your physical and mental experience of relaxation.
The thought, the breath, live with us. Relax and trust yourself, we are aware, we are alive. Like on a mindful journey on the beach, sandy feet, our thoughts come to the shore like waves, carried by the wind. Every wave a thought, just coming to shore and sinking into the ground. Observe and be aware of your breath. Listen. The in and out, equally in, equally out.

Breathe naturally and hear the sounds of the waves. No need to do anything, just be present and aware. Balance your breath and let yourself be safe at shore, trust. Your whole body comes to ease, to peace, to just relax. Observe the vast space of the ocean, the horizon, the endless tide. Coming and going, see the wind carry the waves to shore. Be aware of the nature of the breath. Now maintain this image until even this one is flowing away. A space of peace and balance, every thought we trust, we accept and let be. May there be any sensation, prickling, tingling, vibrating, warm or cold, lightness, numbness, any sensation, any thought, any wave, just observe and see it coming and going, like the breath. Pain, sorrow, hardship,

just a thought, as it comes and goes, so impermanent, so it comes to shore, and we smile. Smile in gratitude, in peace, in joy. Ease in. Relax.
Evenly breathe and deepen your breathing. Inhale. Exhale, and see the body be just a body, see the mind just as it is. Observe the depths of the breath. Rising and passing away. Rising and passing away. Ease in. Relax.

Becoming aware of relaxation

This is a meditation where you will rest in awareness. By doing so you can consciously start to become more aware of the sensations that accompany relaxation.

Find the ease, be aware of the breathing naturally flowing, be aware of every sensation of the body. Wherever a sensation arises be sure it passes eventually. Whatever it is; Tingling, Prickling, Vibrating, Warmth, Cold, lightness, numbness, whatever it may be, be sure it passes eventually. Just observe and see that you don't label it, be aware that whatever and wherever it happens, it is just happening in the moment. May All sensations be equally observed. Equally with a balanced mind.

A mind that is resting on awareness, a still mind that is actively attentive, a mind that knows all the patterns. Rising and passing away, a constant coming and going, impermanent, ever changing. The nature of the sensations is there to transform. Just relax and observe the changes, the rising and passing away, the nature of impermanence. Keep yourself calm, keep a still and balanced mind. Equal at any time.

Breathe evenly, in and out. Evenly observe any sensation with a balanced mind. With a calm and equanimous mind. Still there might be sensations that make us feel in a way and it is all ok, just go with the feeling for awhile, befriend it, trust it, be even and do not judge or label it. As it is a part of your life it surely has its place. Give it space, let it rest, let it be and feel free. An endless lake of awareness, so still, so calm, so beautiful. Any ripple is to be observed, and when the mind is so quiet, than we may have a glance to the bottom of the lake.

There we may see our life, just as it is. See it with an equanimous mind, always aware and attentive. Balanced and calm mind. In the stillness we can see. In the beauty we feel free. Every sensation, every thought, let it be, relax and breathe.

Cultivating relaxation - This meditation has specifically been designed to assist you to cultivate relaxation. Purposefully practising relaxing makes it an easy state to enter at will.

Whenever you feel agitated, out of balance and Harmony, see the truth as it is. Every moment is ever-changing and impermanent. Every sensation is ever in transformation. Every thought comes and goes, nothing is here to stay, except our divine peace and happiness. Practice this divine peace and happiness and all the imbalance will fade, pass away to change into absolute equanimity. By the practice with focus on the object of the breath, we attentively watch our friend. Our breath is accompanying us every moment of our life and therefore we come back to the breath. To be present. To be alive. We keep our focus with the breathing to stay present and harmonious, with breath, there comes Life.

There is life within awareness. Is the breathing calm and equal, the awareness can travel peacefully with our life. Is the flow of breath in peace, our life likewise is. Therefore focus on the breathing, patiently and persistently, observing, seeing the everlasting changes and be aware of all the sensations. Whatever arises will come and go, rise and pass away. Focus on the small area from the upper lip to the nostrils and watch the breath moving in, and moving out again. Intensely inhale once and maintain the focus on that part of the face, with absolute awareness of the breath. Maintain and cultivate awareness of the breath, befriend it and let it be the friend for life, evenly flowing, naturally growing our sense of Self. Trust that there is Harmony and Peace, know that the breath is there. Relax and breathe.

In a Single moment of uncertainty, find truth in the reality of life. Breathing is real and essential. Breathe and evenly, patiently give yourself the trust to be your own master. Practice diligently and cultivate mastery over the breathing. In and out, equally, evenly, in balance and Harmony, we can be. Practice patiently and persistently. Breathe equanimously. Relax.

Reflecting upon relaxation - What does it mean to relax? Where do you go to the relax? What do you do to relax? Sit in reflection in this meditation session and contemplate the meaning of relaxation.

Sit with an equanimous mind. Start again the practice and remind yourself. Remind your senses of the peace and harmony of relaxation. Remember all the moments of joy that make you feel in balance. Imbalance comes from habit, so think and focus on habits that make you feel relaxed... make up an image of yourself, smiling and at peace. Where this place is, only you personally know, only one Self knows truly. See yourself sitting, smiling, simplifying. To see yourself in relaxation, to observe a thought and to know it's truth. Do you spend time with your friend, the breath, the everlasting bond to life, or do you do something else? Do you go to the beach, the Forest or to the mountains to see yourself happy, at peace, in relaxation?

Whatever you do, practice makes it happen, so what you practice every day makes your life. So? Think of the best moments of joy and happiness, be aware of the great joys in life. Smile and remember the upbeat, heartfelt moments of bliss. Smile and dissolve into the divine peace & harmony. Breathe and feel alive. Relax. Give thanks, give appreciation and gratitude to your Self. Your breath, your thoughts, your sensations all are here for your life. Reflect your life in the stillness of awareness.

Allow yourself to dwell in peace, in mind and thought. Contemplate on the true essence of relaxation. Practice, master and cultivate all you need for a life of yours. With the power of the breath and the equanimity of mind, we connect to all living beings, to all the universe, to the truth within our Self. Be true to yourself, relax and trust the breath. Breathe and smile gently, feel the balance within body, mind and Soul. Come once more back to the sound of breathing and listen in. Be aware. Meditate. Relax.

<u>The upwards journey along the spine</u>

We journey into our body to discover the vast possibility of our spine, the Axis of the Universe. Together we traverse many lands to find a heavenly gate.

We imagine our spine as a ladder to heaven. The spine is an endless possibility to travel with awareness along this mystical path to freedom.

Everyone finds a comfortable seat. As we feel the Ground our body becomes naturally adjusted to the earth. As we sit we make sure our buttocks is equally balanced on both sides. Left and right, yang and yin are in harmony. We come to ease closing our eyes and imagining our being safely surrounded by a bubble of shimmering golden light. (Sound from singing bowl, gong)

See the bubble around you and be aware that this bubble protects, nurtures and allows you to travel everywhere in in your mind. So as we are all set, we prepare to visit one of the most important places of our human body, some call it the Axis of the Universe, it is that important - the spine.

First feel the spine as you sit and breathe.

We inhale, gently breathe and let the air travel to the ground you are sitting on. Visualize the very Fundament of your being, the core, the ground. Here, everything is still, like an infinite sea of energy. We travel with our golden light bubble to this land and sit on the lake, so beautiful and pristine. See the lake, does it sit still and quiet, or does it ripple waves? Observe and be aware, the stillness is essential.

So we can witness the life air.

Breathe in and out.

Streaming in, the air flows downwards, breathing out we see the motion upwards.

Repeat this breathing for a while and watch the lake, what is happening to it?

Breathe in, let the air settle in, breathe out, let it rise.

While we find ourselves safe in the Golden Light Bubble, we witness the reflection of the sun, right on this lake. The beautiful glitter, sparkling and endlessly moving.

The lake is like a mirror for the sky, the beautiful shining of heavens light up above.

While we look into the horizon We see a mystical bird using the upwards air to hover in a vortex to the sky. The graceful beauty and stunning ease of the birds wings make us free and we join the bird. We get closer and closer to the wind vortex, and slowly step into the air moving up. Light like a bird we move up. Like God has given us wings we hover with the warm air to a new height. Slowly ascending, we lift to the peaks of mountains, looking over the land. Look and see the trees, green and lush, see the lake peacefully floating, be aware of the suns light. Our golden bubble protects us and keeps us safe. Even in midst the body, vertebrae by vertebrae, breath by breath we gently come into harmony and alignment.

Coming closer to the Sky.

Our wings are getting stronger, our breath is heavier. Breathe intense. Let it out through the mouth and continue on. Relax the jaw, feel free to lay down, make yourself comfortable as we are slowly approaching a magnificent golden gate with a guardian, strong and fierce he greets us.

It is the Heartkeeper who knows us, smiles and welcomes us in devotion. We put our hands together, bow and greet him with a smile. We stop close to Him and observe His form. Like a hero, a legendary warrior for peace, he says: Follow the Air and the Sun, now your journey has only begun. Enter and find the Palast of your heart, this one is all a kingdom longing to serve the good.

Smile, be happy and enjoy.
The Heartkeeper bows again and opens this huge golden gate, we enter in, within.

Lift up your chin, let the focus be on the nose tip, and breathe. This is the Garden of Heaven, a Kingdom for Good, a Palast for You. Everything in here is true and meant to be for you.
Give yourself a moment to hold this image and repeat:
I am safe and sound I am safe and sound I am safe and sound
You be safe and sound You be safe and sound You be safe and sound
We are safe and sound We are safe and sound We are safe and sound
Relax and take a seat on your throne, a golden throne overlooking all the land. Rely on the golden light that protects, and send it back all the way. Let the golden light sink into the smallest, even tiniest part of the world. Every little piece shall be fulfilled. So the golden light shines throughout the world and illuminates every house, every village, every city and everyone's home.
(Have a candle or light inside)
Now you can imagine everyone happy and fulfilled with the light from your throne. Now you can visualize a little smile on everyone's face as you see the Heartkeepers smile.

Now let the whole Axis of the Universe shine with golden light and see the stars, the galaxies and cosmic entities be nurtured with this light. As we now see all the universes illuminated, we can now illuminate this room.
(Play soothing music preferably gong, singing bowl)
Slowly and gently we come to our private universe, gently we come with awareness to our bodies, smoothly we breathe and let the life air fulfill us with love and light.

Rub your palms to create warmth on each side, rub and put them on your face. Let them be like a warming bath in bliss. Smile and enjoy. The hands can now spread this bliss all over the body, all over, especially there where it is needed.
Feel free to sigh of relief.
HAAA, HUUU, HMMM
Come to the here and now.
Fold your hands and bow.
Make a sound like wooow.
Open your eyes, give thanks, Namaste

Meditation for Deep Sleep:

Prepare yourself for a deep relaxation of body mind and spirit. This meditation will include a full body relaxation where we start from the head bringing awareness to the bottom of the feet, scanning and relaxing the whole body. While relaxing the whole body, the mind might wander Yet one might focus on the breath and the part where the breathing goes into the nostrils, to maintain awareness. When the mind wanders we can always come back to the breath.

Gently and naturally be aware of the breath coming in and going out. You are a life and you can be thankful to be a life. While preparing just bring your body in a relaxed posture preferably laying down on your back having your legs shoulder width apart and the hands on the side of the body palms facing up. One might be covered with a blanket and cushioned with a pillow on the necessary parts.
This is a deep relaxation, so you might be able to lose your focus and to be in total tranquillity for the whole time of this meditation.

Let's start by relaxing the whole body, from the head, you feel the top of the head, just relax the head. You feel the forehead and the muscles around the eyes, now let go of the pressure around the eyes, around the jaw, along the mouth, just letting go of all the pressure relaxing with every single breath.
Just relax your throat, breathe, and just relax your shoulders.
Imagine all the weight from your shoulders lightens with every breath.
The way of the breath lightens the whole being and you come to the arms bringing awareness to them. Be aware of the arms and the arms are relaxing. The elbows and wrists are equally relaxing with every breath. You are noticing the hands and the palms of the hands, and with the awareness the hands relax.

With the awareness, constantly breathing, the chest will relax. Just keep the breathing and stay equanimous, with the breathing the inner organs will relax. Feel the breath coming in into the lungs, around the heart and all around the body. Now be aware of the belly, breathing and feeling the belly relaxes with every breath. One is sinking into the ground becoming heavier and heavier and letting go of all the stress and pressure. All the tension dissolves into air or finds its grounding into the floor.

It is all energy. With the relaxation the energy can flow and harmonize with the ground and with the energy around you. In the air and in the earth there's balance. This balance is spreading all around the belly, around the chest and around the head. With every breath the relaxation is sinking deeper and deeper into Ones being. Even all the muscles around the hips and at the bottom of your spine, are now with awareness and relaxing.

Ones attention is the root of energy, now at the spine. This is where peace and harmony as well as deep relaxation stem. Here, we can imagine a beautiful, lush red flower blooming and showing the blossom of wonderful red petals spreading into every direction, equally the relaxation is spreading evenly in the whole body.

One relaxes legs and knees, the lower thighs and ankles as well as the feet, are now filled with awareness. We breathe into this and with the awareness and the breath you are bringing relaxation. This relaxation spreads even into the tippy toes. Here we let the energy rise again and we just notice and be aware of all the body parts.

Whatever sensation arises we stay evenly in balance. Notice the legs, fully notice the legs and relax. Notice the hips at the bottom of the spine, fully notice the hips at the bottom of the spine, and relax. Notice the lower back and fully notice every vertebrae of the spine and relax. Notice the upper back and fully notice the neck and the back of the head. Relax and sink deeper and deeper with every single breath, the body becomes lighter and lighter. The whole body is now light and one can feel the blossom of the flower, so light the whole body is equally relaxed from the head to the toes, the relaxation spreads from the belly into every cell of the body.

The whole body is rooted in relaxation and bliss. A beautiful light grounds one from bottom of the spine and the red flower turns into a beautiful flower of light protecting one from head to toe. Sheltering one for a good, deep relaxation. Equally breathe and feel the breath relaxing one from the head to the toe, all surrounded by a protective light. Whenever one feels ready, the breath can take us deeper or it can release the relaxation, just notice again the body parts and see how every body part is awakening with the energy of the breathing, coming and going, we focus on the entrance of the nose again and help ourselves to a nice massage or soothing music.

<u>Body Scan</u>

Come to full relaxation by giving yourself space. The whole body is on the ground. The whole body relaxes. Breathe through, sigh of relief and feel the firm ground. Nothing you need to do, nowhere you need to go, just relax and feel the sensations of your body. Be aware that this is Yoga Nidra, the conscious sleep. Stay aware by listening deeply to the voice. As we go through the different parts of the body with our awareness, we stay awake. The body relaxes fully and we close our eyes. Remain aware of the natural flow of respiration. The natural flow coming in and out. Coming in and flowing out. Feel the sensations, whatever it may be, vibrating, tingling, itching, warmth or cold, lightness or numbness, whatever it may be, you remain aware of the natural breath, entering on the nose tip. Let the breath flow and whenever you lose yourself in thoughts, come back to the breath entering in and out. We start scanning and wandering with our awareness from head to feet. By doing so we relax.

Start to be aware of the top of your head, feel the top of the head, relax the top of the head, the top of the head is relaxed. Let the awareness sink slowly into the skull area, the back of the head and into the face. Be aware, feel and relax. Be aware of the forehead, the nostrils, the jaw, the mouth and chin. Feel every little part and let go. Relax. Be aware of the shoulders and neck area, around the throat. Feel the whole shoulder girdle, the neck area and throat. Be aware and feel, any sensation we just observe, just observe, feel and relax. The head area we relax, relax the whole head area of the body. Let the awareness sink into the chest area, around the heart, feel and be aware of the tiny muscles evenly pumping blood into the heart, be aware of the rhythm of your breathing and your heart beat. Observe and feel any sensation coming up. Give space and relax all the chest area, all the chest is relaxed.

Balance Meditation

Find a comfortable seat, bringing your whole body into balance between earth and sky. You can sit or lay on the ground in a comfortable place. Watch your breath coming equally in and out. Working with the breath is the one fundamental trust, as we live, we breathe.

Come to terms with your body, come to ease, settle, there is nothing to fear, relax, with a voice that is guiding you into meditation.
Just trust the breathing as it is coming and going, gently notice the breath and be aware of the sensation of the breath entering the nostrils and leaving them again.

Equally in and out again, breathe and be aware how it comes into your nose tip, into your body and into your heart.

Here in the heart the breath is home. The beloved invites the lover and everything comes home. One can notice there is awareness in the breath which is bringing us home into the body and into the heart.

One notices every part of the body, from the heart to the belly, to the spine, to the shoulders and head, and even to the tippy toes. Feel how the heart is opening and chest is widening. Here in the heart is where the eternal spark of light resides.

Breathe out all you are letting go and receive all you breathe in. One can make up a thought, we are letting go, and we can make up a thought that we receive, therefore we can inhale I Am Trust, and exhale all that we are not. Breathe, in I am Trust and breathe out again. Continue on and know that the thought and words travel with the breath, into your heart.

Find peace and relax the body, coming to a state of trust and harmony.

With every single breath one is becoming lighter and lighter. I am Light travels with the breath and comes into every cell of the body. The whole body is now very light and even so light it starts to float and lifting of the ground, just with the help of the breath.

The body is so light and trusting the body floats into the space of Trust, the whole body is now fully in a space of trust and peace. Feel the ease, the small breeze from the air entering the nose and coming to the heart.

In our imagination one can see a nice tender space where we can land again for good care, like in a flower field, full of moss and soft ground, landing there it feels like we are home in a space of trust and balance.

Feel the balance of the breath, equally inhaling and exhaling, as the thoughts arise we can just notice them like one notices the leaves dancing in the wind.

See the beautiful wind playing with the trees, also these trees are giving us shelter and equanimity, just trust and find a nice space close to that tree.

The trees are holding up the earth and likewise we can hold trust within us, just steady and always growing up towards the sky.

Embrace nature and feel the rhythm of the breath, find the heart and maybe there is a friend who likes to join us.

Do you have a friend you like to see? Invite this friend with a smile into your light space of heart.

To trust means to have full faith in goodness in person.

Whatever will be, everything turns out just for a reason. Therefore, always be thankful and happy for all the little things. Even watch the flowers who are so happily growing on the field providing nectar for the bees, and see the trees?

Do they ever complain? Still and steady they hold on for days and days on end, especially when there is a good friend. Walking along the small stream, the water is crystal clear and there is a fish or two within the river that flows into a lake.
 Finding a reflection in the lake, one can see a mirror face of the wonderful surface, within this endless space.

Holding the moment of trust, even when there is no doubt, no lack and desire to be somewhere else, that is balance and trust.

Giving a hand to someone, and see there is a smile that illuminates the world, that is trust. Even together or just being alone, that is trust. Know to be content even when there is a surprising event, like a dancing tree.

Without any fault everything finds a place on this earthly surface, even the rain. All come the same, yet we trust and have everything we need. A shelter is right there. All in care, just trust and see, everything is in divine harmony.

Life is miraculous and wonderful as sometimes unexplainably we just trust and see the magic unfold within the matter of the now, breathing and opening our hearts for the grace of goodness, one shall receive the mercy of the light.

In Peace, Love and Unity, knowing everything is in divine harmony. Breathe equally.

Notice the subtle sensation of the thoughts and the breath coming to terms with the light, knowing everything shall be alright. The perfect harmony is here, within the heart of everyone.

The flowers and the trees, the friends and families all together like to live in harmonies. All are the same in their goal to come back home.

Where the heart is there is bliss, and all longing to never miss a chance of meeting someone new, just trust and what we will do? Smile and breathe, greet as a friend always and forever one to be.

Then, all shall be happy.

Within the whole body there is now the light of trust spreading and we can know that all living entities are seeking the same light of trust, and trust is everywhere and there and within the heart. Like there is air within the space there is love for all in the face of a smiling heart.

We are all a part of this world. Even when the sun sets for a goodbye it shall still shine, let's embrace the stillness of the lake one more time and see the setting suns face shining for a good night over the hills and within the heart, all we are a part.

This space is here and now for us to feel, from the tippy-toes to the head, to the chest and all around the nose, with the jaw and around the neck, the arms, shoulders and hands are relaxed, as well as the finger tips and the lips, the jaw and the neck.

The whole body is filled with lightness and trust, as we breathe there is no must, but we can do, whatever there is to do! We can also trust! Where there is no must, just let be, and feel free to also renounce and come back home to the premises of the body where the soul finds its heart.

There, everything is a start and we begin to breathe.
Be aware of the breath and let it flow naturally, just be aware of the body and relax from the head to the toes. The sunshine is now all gone, yet one can see the reflection within the sky, that is coming in beautiful colours and o 'wonder why we deserve to be blessed. Of course, because we trust.

Let's adjust the body to find a comfortable way, of trusting our close ones each and everyday, maybe invite them for a dream with the heart-full space of trust, giving oneself to the best.

Give thanks and appreciation to the best ones close by, and be grateful for every single breath, as it comes naturally, we give thanks to nature accordingly.
All the appreciation to the world family.

May all beings be happy and live in equanimity.

Meditations for Overthinking

Just sit in a comfortable position and come to ease.
The best solution for overthinking is proper grounding. Earthing or grounding happens naturally through proper posture and breathing. One can walk bare feet on the beach or in the forest also, but best grounding happens naturally within the heart, and especially in a group of like-minded people.

It is also recommended to search out a meditation group and to create a sacred space for communal meditation. This is meditation is for individuals and groups, to relieve and restore awareness of thoughts and words, according to balance and harmony. Balance and harmony are the basis of ones good life, in peace and happiness. This is due to the nature of energy. Energy always remains equal and in balance. Energy is also conserved equally and fully in harmony with life.

Breathing means to transform energies, from oxygen to carbon dioxide, from Neutral energy to energy fueling the body, heart and mind. This energy is spiritual in nature, meaning, it is always constant and eternal. Try to get a grasp of this:

We are living on a tiny globe of water, earth and other natural elements floating in the middle of the space called the Milky Way, which is again in tiny dimension to the whole cosmos of multiple universes and infinite stars and suns. On this tiny planet earth, oneself makes up a minute fragment of history and population, yet one thinks to be the centre of existence.

See the bigger picture. The whole cosmos, the suns, stars, moons, planets and the planet earth. Most of it is all within empty space, or unmanifested matter. This gives a frame to the picture of the universal thought, of the existence, the universe and own thinking.
Be happy, to breathe and to live, nonetheless, you are alive and fully aware, breathing and knowing to be.

Breathe equally in and out again. Breathe and find ease within the sitting posture. This sitting posture shall be align with earth and sky. The spine shall be in alignment with neck and buttocks. The buttocks is firmly situated on the ground or mat, and the neck is in one straight line with the upper body. Neck and shoulders are relaxed and the head is relaxed, slightly gazing towards the nose tip.
Focus here. Breathe and notice the breathing streaming into the nostrils and streaming out again. Notice the breath streaming into the space of lungs and hearts.
Here, the air can circulate and find space in between the alveoli and little gaps and niches.

'Like a lamp in a windstill place doesn't flicker, the meditator keeps unwavering in his focus of mind and consciousness.' (Bhagavād-Gita, 6.19)

Sit still and breathe equally. Focus on the nose-tip and straight over the lip, where the entrance of the nose happens to be. Let the air flow naturally and notice any slight sensation. Be aware of any sensation, may it be tickling, vibrating, throbbing, warmth or cold. Whatever it may be, just be aware of it and let it pass.

As it arises, it shall pass. There is constant balance within, and no duality of matter can distract one from focusing on the nose tip.

Keep the breathing equal and focus now your attention to the space where the heart resides. See a beautiful luminous personality right here, residing within the heart of ones consciousness, and also within the physical heart. See this unique personality. See it clearly and be aware of its form and character.

See the blissful smile and moonlike face, see the beauty within every part, from the feet to the head. Within the heart there is a sacred space full of lotus flowers and magnificent trees that shelter this personality. Be aware of the breathing, equally streaming in and out again. Notice the wind dancing within the leaves of the tree. Notice the eternal personality residing within the heart. Full of bliss and joy, this eternal personality pervades all the hearts. Even when this personality goes through youth, growth and old age, it doesn't change.

There is a mirror lake and when one looks into its reflection, then one can easily notice that bodies might change, from youth, to old age, but one can always say: 'This is Me'.

One can always say: 'I am who I am', at any stage of life. Bodies might change, but the personality remains equally situated within the heart of eternity and wisdom.

Every though is like a ripple on this lake of consciousness. The reflection, of course, gets irritated by the subtle wave of thought. Yoga, hence, is the method to still this lake of consciousness to still the mind and to experience balance and equanimity, as distributed by Patanjali in the Yoga Sutras.

Breathe equally, and notice the waves of thought. All the thoughts rippling on the surface of the lake are due to identification with the matter of self. This self identifies with 'I am English, I am American, Australian, British, I am Christian, Muslim, Hindu, I am rich, I am poor, and so on. From this Identification all the thoughts find expression and give ripples to the still lake of consciousness.

Incessant thoughts trouble the mind due to material nature, and they come and come again, like waves on the ocean. However, if one identifies with eternal truths, then, this lake of consciousness can be stilled.

Thinking in eternal and not temporary means links one up to the absolute Truth, which is eternal. In the scriptures it is stated that the Absolute Truth is a Person and that this person has a form of eternity, wisdom and bliss. As soon as one identifies ones individuality with this eternal person, one becomes practically linked up to the consciousness of grace or God.

This absolute, Supreme Truth is the best remedy for all thoughts, and thoughts can be beneficial, if directly correctly to the Supreme Source, or Eternal Light, God, Heavenly Father, or Supreme Personality.

Ones simple, minute and independent personality can thus be linked up to the Supreme Person, who is wholeness, abundance and balance. This link brings balance and peace of mind.

Actually, every thought can be wonderful, in the service of the Supreme Truth. However, controlling the thoughts and mind is very difficult, however one can practice stilling the lake of consciousness through meditation and yoga.

By chanting the Maha-Mantra, or Supreme Chant for Deliverance Hare Krsna Hare Krsna Krsna Krsna Hare Hare/ Hare Rama Hare Rama Rama Rama Hare Hare, one can still the mind perfectly and bring overthinking into halt. This, the thoughts are reconnected to the Supreme source, giving energy a proper channel to facilitate change. This might take practice but next to breathing, chanting is the perfect way to overcome overthinking.

Just chant according to prescribed words:

Hare Krsna
Hare Krsna
Krsna Krsna
Hare Hare
Hare Rāma
Hare Rāma
Rāma Rāma
Hare Hare

Repeat and keep on repeating this mantra. Breathing comes naturally by speaking these sacred thirty-two syllables, literally referring to the Supreme Personality, Krsna, to the Energy of the Supreme, namely Hari, and the source of all pleasure, literally Rāma.

This Mantra translates to: 'O divine Energy, O Supreme Person, O Source of All Pleasure, please deliver this One from Overthinking.'

This Mantra is actually good for all matters of material distractions, disturbances and calamities. It works perfect as a prayer, and wonderful in a group meditation.

All over the World people chant this mantra effectively and with great results.

Just be humble and happy.

This could be your last day on earth, or it is just the start of a new life. Who knows what is tomorrow and what will be in the future. There is only one moment to live, fully, aware, and happy.

Breathe and be thankful, to be alive. Leave all the sorrow and grief aside, and chant. Meditate and breathe. Be happy.

While sitting, in any circumstances, one can be aware of mercy. Just open up the palms and make sure to breathe equally. Gaze towards the sky and witness a glaring light of hope and grace streaming from the eternal blissful sky flowing into ones heart. This life of awareness is with the matter of the breath. Consciousness, or the light of awareness, travels with the breath. Be aware of it, embrace and give thanks. Life is beautiful and so one is.

Notice that every breath is unique and wonderful.

While breathing one can practice detachment from any false identification. This body one is carrying around is just a temporary vessel bound to birth, growth, disease, decay and death. This mind also, is just an accumulation of thoughts, therefore body and mind are temporary. What remains? Only the spiritual soul, the spark of eternity is everlasting. When the practitioner thus identifies with the eternal spiritual soul, one becomes liberated from the bondage of birth and death.

'The embodied spiritual soul transmigrates through boyhood, youth and old age, similarly, the spiritual spark changes bodies at the moment of death. A sober person is not affected by such a change.' (Bhagavad-Gita, 2.14)

One can be sobering the mind and body, as well as cleansing the image of true self. One can finally see the blissful, eternal form of ones true nature. This finishes all over-thinking due to the realization of ones own true nature.

Therefore, use the breath to practice detachment. Inhale, and exhale. Equally and rhythmically. Now, keep in breathing. Just add a thought to every breath. With inhale, generate the thought 'I am not this temporary body', exhale and find relief. With the next inhale generate the thought: 'I am not this temporary mind'.

Keep breathing and focus the thought and inhale: 'I am not this body', exhale and release. Inhale with the thought: 'I am not this mind'. Exhale and release. Let go of all breathing and feel for a moment. Let the breathing be natural.

This can be practiced for 3-5 minutes while just focusing on the negation of this temporary body, one can also add thoughts of positivity: 'I am eternal' or 'I am bliss'.

Now, we start again, inhaling 'I am eternal', exhaling and releasing. Inhaling 'I am bliss', and exhaling . Release and relax. Continue breathing naturally.

This time we combine both and make a full circle of twelve breaths:

Inhale: I am Eternal
Exhale: I am not this body
Inhale: I am Bliss
Exhale: I am not this mind.

Repeat twelve times.

Inhale: I am Eternal
Exhale: I am not this body
Inhale: I am Bliss
Exhale: I am not this mind.

Inhale: I am Eternal
Exhale: I am not this body
Inhale: I am Bliss
Exhale: I am not this mind.

Inhale: I am Eternal
Exhale: I am not this body
Inhale: I am Bliss
Exhale: I am not this mind.

Inhale: I am Eternal
Exhale: I am not this body
Inhale: I am Bliss
Exhale: I am not this mind.

Inhale: I am Eternal
Exhale: I am not this body
Inhale: I am Bliss
Exhale: I am not this mind.

Inhale: I am Eternal
Exhale: I am not this body
Inhale: I am Bliss
Exhale: I am not this mind.

Half way, can you notice the breathe being aligned and in balance?

Back to awareness.

Inhale: I am Eternal
Exhale: I am not this body
Inhale: I am Bliss
Exhale: I am not this mind.

Inhale: I am Eternal
Exhale: I am not this body
Inhale: I am Bliss
Exhale: I am not this mind.

Inhale: I am Eternal
Exhale: I am not this body
Inhale: I am Bliss
Exhale: I am not this mind.

Inhale: I am Eternal
Exhale: I am not this body
Inhale: I am Bliss
Exhale: I am not this mind.

Inhale: I am Eternal
Exhale: I am not this body
Inhale: I am Bliss
Exhale: I am not this mind.

Inhale: I am Eternal
Exhale: I am not this body
Inhale: I am Bliss
Exhale: I am not this mind.

Relax and Release in normal breathing. Let it be natural and come to ease.

This is actual and eternal realization of ones spiritual nature. Spiritual in nature means to be distinctly aware of ones temporary nature consisting of body and mind, and at the same time to identify with an eternal, and blissful truth.

This truth resides with everyone, within every heart of every living being. This is confirmed in scriptures, like 'the kingdom of God is within' or 'sarvasya hrdi caham sannivisto' (Bhagavad-Gita, 15.15): The Absolute Truth is situated within everyone's heart.

This is pure thinking and so one can be sobered from material and temporary conditioning.

We all have fantastic capabilities to be conscious, and this is truly ones true occupation as a living human being, to be conscious, and finally to be conscious of the Absolute Truth.

Thoughts that are overwhelming and disturbing are also due to attachment. Attachment to the material world begins with the senses, and namely the tongue. The tongue is the most ferocious of all sense organs and because the tongue is so attached to talking and eating, one becomes deeply entangled in sense gratification. This attachment of satisfying the senses is limiting, disturbing and agitating.

Likewise, one constantly thinks about sex life, gambling, eating flesh of dead animals and how to get high. This is degrading the mind and consciousness. This is misuse of human life. Overthinking is based on attachment, and from attachment lust, greed and anger arise. Thus, thoughts steadily crave for sense gratification.

This can be controlled. The sense organs must be controlled, and especially the tongue. With two simple methods, one can still the tongue, and thus the mind, anger, lust and attachment.

One method we have already discussed: Taking to the chanting of Hare Krsna Hare Krsna Krsna Krsna Hare Hare/ Hare Rama Hare Rama Rama Rama Hare Hare can purify the senses and bring proper use to the tongue. This mantra helps to release tension and to properly redirect thoughts, words and equally breathing.

This is actually the best way.
However, while conscious of ones breathing, and maybe in a situation of Stress one can put the tongue on the roof of the mouth. The tip of the tongue thereby touches the upper part of the cave of the mouth. Here one can hold the tongue and press it against the roof. This helps to stimulate the brain and nerves within the skull. The tongue is very strong. Be careful and like a animal dompteur is conquering a wild beast by using certain tools and elements. One can use this technique to still the mind, however it is better to engage the tongue in proper chanting of the Maha-Mantra.

Eventually, one can find a proper on-site teacher or temple where Yoga Meditation or especially Bhakti-Yoga is practiced and thus experiencing the remedy for overthinking.

Try to continue with the breathing exercise above. Detaching from the temporary mind and body, to witness the soul within.

One can now relax and come onto a dream journey.

Relax, one is safe and in a sacred space. Sitting on a still lake, very subtle and soft, the water is tranquil and one can witness the vibration of peace. The winds are dancing within the leaves and one might experience sensations of quietness and calm. Let the mind calm and see the lake of consciousness.

There are plenty of beautiful lotus flowers swimming on the lake. Did you know that whatever happens, Lotus flowers always stay pure and untouched? No dirt, rain or swamp can touched the beauty of the Lotus. It's petals are magnificently crafted by nature for purity, layers with film of transparent grace, the lotus is never affected by any space.

See the swans playing within the Lotus which glow in a soothing and purple glow. The white swans are very beautiful and somehow it looks funny how swans play, but at the same time elegant as well. Yet, the Lotus stays untouched and still. There are some ripples on the lake, but no worry, one is safely protected at shore, sitting under a great tree.

Find ease and witness the stillness of the lake and the purity of lotus flowers. Watch the swans play and the wind dance within the leaves. Keep breathing naturally, noticing the breath and being aware of it at any time. Always stay present and awake. So, one can follow along. Breathe equally in and out again.

Keep the breathing going and keep an equanimous mind. With all one has learnt, keep remembering; it is all a constant coming and going, rising and passing again.

Once you focus on the nose-tip or on the heart, one can stay equally disposed and balanced, no matter what happens, one remains in perfect balance through focus.

When the focus shifts and still thoughts are coming, then one can use the Maha-Mantra Hare Krsna Hare Krsna Krsna Krsna Hare Hare Hare Rama Hare Rama Rama Rama Hare Hare to still the mind. Silently or loudly. One can chant it as long as one wants.

And to really work only the overthinking one can practice detachment, focusing the breath and thoughts together:

Inhale: I am Eternal
Exhale: I am not this body
Inhale: I am Bliss
Exhale: I am not this mind.

Eventually, practice makes perfect, and one can notice results best after 48 days of practice. Therefore, continue and stay steady. Keep on breathing and notice the breath. Notice the sensations, and dream away.

Be surrounded by a beautiful light, shining and glimmering from the heart space, surrounding one in full bliss and eventually protecting one from any contamination. This protective light might surround you always and keeps you steady within calamities. Just call out for protection whenever needed. Be aware of the breathing and let this glowing light of protection spread into the whole world.

May this protective light with all beings, all alike.

Fully rest and relax.

Meditations for Self-Love

<u>The source within the Heart</u>

Breathe and be aware of the heart space. Here, in the heart, all energies meet and create balance. Balance is key for Meditation.

One can have balance through an equanimous sitting position, and according to the matter of the breath.

Balance is like a mountain. Very firm and steady.
Just be a mountain, and whatever comes, thoughts, distractions, itching, trembling, pain, just be steady and keep the meditation very equally and peacefully.

Just inhale and be aware of the little pause between the in-and out-breath. Be aware of the subtle sensation of the breath moving into the nostrils and moving out again. Just simply be steady and aware, that the breath is connecting us to all the life. In consciousness, there is no difference between gold, stone, wood, water, and other things. They are all-natural matter. Even sensations like tickling, itching, vibrating, warmth, cold, are all the same, rising and passing.

Like a wind sweeps over the land and makes many trees dance, but the mountain remains steady. Be that mountain. A mountain is a steady magnet. Just attract goodness, by being a magnet for pure goodness. Uttering sacred syllables and affirmations help to get through the storm, yet one has to focus and face any difficulty. Easily, then one attracts beauty, wealth, fame, wisdom and so on.

Just breathe equally and hold the key balance. Sit on the feet of the Supreme Balance in Person and be aware of the heart. Here, within the heart wonders are happening. By breathing consciousness travels along the channels of energy from the outside to the inside. Within, in the heart, the air can unfold and circulate. Here, balance finds its expression. Notice the little pause even so after the exhale. Stillness takes care of the necessary space within the heart and the flowers of the garden of the heart can blossom to attract nectar-hunting honey bees.

Just be aware of the inhale, equal, and the exhale, equal. Find yourself in this wonderful space where the grass is very soft and lush, there are colourful cows grazing peacefully on the field and one can see the juicy green fields along the garden where nice desire trees are cultivated.

A gardener takes good care of all the plants by removing the weeds of ignorance. By conscious breathing one can, little by little, remove these weeds to get rid of fatigue, greed, pride, envy, and lust. This garden is a sacred space to meditate and there is even so the everlasting lake of consciousness just in near sight. A sunny morning provides wonderful and auspicious perspectives of the sunlight reflecting the whole spectrum of colours.

Notice the lake of consciousness and be aware of its state. Is it still? Is it fickle? How is this pure lake behaving? Slowly lean towards the lake and see your reflection within the waters. How are you seeing yourself?

Reflect and contemplate, lean back and relax within the meditative garden of your heart. Here, one can also plant the seed of good fortune. By addressing the divine feminine, the aspect of you that sets free fertility and purity.

Be aware of the subtle sound of the breathing and just remain like the steady mountain beyond the fields and meadows. The garden is waiting for a special seed, a desire-seed.

So, whatever you desire, you can cultivate. It takes time to plant, but at the right moment, one can implement a good seed in good soil.

Whatever you wish for, be clear about it, check it and nurture this wish like your little child. Be aware of this phenomenon that brings life to sprout. Whatever it may be, hold your hands together and think about a seed that likes to grow.

One can plant abundance, happiness and wealth, by giving all these to the Supreme Balance offering it with love.
 'Please, let this desire-seed sprout into wealth, abundance and happiness.'
Then, one can put it into the ground of the hearts garden.

Just envision how a simple seed can grow into a full blossom tree, full of lively blossoms and an abundance of life fruits. Just see the shapes, colours and luminescence emanating from that growing tree. However, it needs time to ripe, the desire can sprout very wonderfully.

Breathe and be equipoised just knowing that everything is already in place. Similar to a tree, one needs to find deep roots in meditation to attract pure fruitful results.

Love Attraction: Offering and Receiving Love

If it would be sold in a shop everyone would buy it. Love. It comes from the heart and is the essential force that connects us humans, person to person. Its divine quality is bliss and truthfulness.

So, just sit under that desire tree and imagine yourself to be very nicely situated in a peaceful. mode of observance. Seeing the cows grazing on the field, listening to the birds in the sky and being aware of the subtle sensation of the life air streaming into the nostrils and out again.

Equally, breathe, and feel the touch of the roots. The lower back, buttocks or whole body may be equally touching the ground. Envision an energetic connection with the ground and also with the heart. From the heart, light illuminates the sight and one can see the spring in the garden of one's heart. The tree is giving a nice shelter before the morning sunshine.

By breathing one can consciously access this garden of hearts, where even friends and family can take a rest. Just call out to someone and see the connection to this person. A loved one might be just waiting to be invited. Love is all you need, just connect to your loved one and let the force act. Love is intelligent, natural life force. Just be a channel for this energy and submit. Smile and be happy, because your loved one is just appearing at the entrance of the garden.

Wonderful as it seems, but your friends have no shoes on! Where there is a beautiful lush garden with soft grass, ain't no one needs shoes. Greetings and a warm welcome, there is enough space under the tree. Just feel free and breathe.

It's okay to dream away, however one may be aware of the breath. Whenever there is doubt, fall, or fear, just breathe. Breathing brings balance. 'Here you are invited to wish for a nice fruit', says the desire-tree. Just speak or think it out, what would you like. The desire-tree is providing you and your friend.

Cheesecake ? No problem, the desire-tree is a wish-fulfilling desire-tree and no desire remains open. It can read your mind.

Speaking of the mind. The mind is like a well that can provide the necessary contact for abundance. If you have a full mind-well, well, that's good, because then one can fetch from the mind-well and give away the awareness. Awareness is the potency from a mindful reservoir. When the mind is empty, well, then it is easy to fill up. Is the mind full, well then, one can fetch awareness from this well. Awareness of attention is the attraction towards the sense objects. While. meditating, one can notice these sense objects and senses to attach, and detach. Once there comes a subtle stream of air, it touches the skin, one can feel, but then it fades just like the breeze fades. Same with sound, taste, smell and sight. Of all the senses and sense objects form, shape and colour are the most attractive, especially to the eyes.

This is why one can envision a garden of wonderful trees or one can determinedly stare at the nose-tip. Both has an effect and keeps the mind busy and attached. To detach the mind, one can use the hands, clapping once or twice. This sound is very powerful and overpowers the attached senses easily.

Just consciously attach your mind and focus towards an object of desire, maybe an apple or a banana, or a cheesecake. Put all the energy of attention into the process and remain still, for a moment, let go. Smile, and offer the desired object to your dear friend or loved one. Leave the breathing natural and see.

Mindfulness can be a process of loving transmission. One can even give love to others just by thought. Further, when the mind is engaged in loving transmission connecting to a higher wish or desire, the senses become fixed. Focusing the mind on the nice form of the Supreme Personality, the origin of all abundance.

All the senses are automatically engaged in the service of the mind. Then, smelling can be very inspiring, hearing a wonderful experience, seeing a miraculous occasion, touching a blissful act, and tasting a joyful endeavour.
Mindfulness can lead to abundance by steady application and determination, as well as faith.

In meditation, one can access these realms of subtle energies, like the lake of consciousness. Here, many seeds of desire are stored, and these seeds again act as potential outcomes.

Offer a Smile

Just sit mindfully with your loved one under that tree within the garden of your heart and breathe. Consciously, rhythmically and equal. Find a smile and also offer this to your friend. Love attracts, and the more attention we give, the more on can reciprocate. Just see your friend from the bottom of the sole, to the tippy toes, along the ankles, calves, knees, thighs, and the upper body. How is this loved one dressed, and what special features can you make out? See the upper body and chest, the arms, hands and fingers. Finally, see the neck, chin, jaw and eyes. See the eyes and forehead. Smile gently, and see your loved one as a meditative companion who has always been within the garden of your heart.

This is even how to attract associates, ad loving relationships. We can desire nice friendships and good relations, and of course one can meditate upon these. One who has a spiritual teacher knows, it is best to see from the feet to the head.

Give thanks and appreciate the community. Be aware of this eternal moment within the garden of the heart, underneath that desire tree. Watch the lake of consciousness be very nice and still. The sunshine of the midday is reflecting within the waters stillness and here swans and cranes are playing in the rear.

Beyond the beautiful lake of consciousness, there are mountains of steadiness and determination, and even upon the peaks, one can see a little reflection of the sunshine. Within the trees, there are plenty of flower blossoms and fruits. Many beautiful leaves are dancing within the wind and the sound of birds is most enchanting. The subtle breeze charms with a sweet aroma of forest fruits.

You and your friend are in meditative harmony, just breathing and enjoying. There is nothing to do, there is no must, no stress, just endless happiness. Blissfully, dreams come true, and a slight bluish hue reflects from the lake of consciousness.

A meditative dream bird lands nearby within a forest grove. It is a very colourful bird, with black, purple, silver and blue feathers. Can you guess what kind of bird is this?

Peace: Padala meditation

Find a comfortable seat. Breathe equally in and out, find your ground and balance as you erect your spine. Gently look upwards, open the throat area and relax the shoulders.
Bring both palms together and chant a Mantra for Peace:
Om Shanti Shanti Shanti x3
Close your eyes, open your hands upwards, create a smile and find yourself watching the life air. See the breath moving into the nostrils and out again. See yourself sitting in a nice and lush forest close to a spring. A wonderful soothing sound sparkles next to you and calms your mind. (Play watery sounds) Listen and find ease.

While we sit in this forest we can hear the sounds of birds (play sounds of birds) and there comes a beautiful peacock, gracefully stepping out of the forest.

A shimmering blue feather cloak opens and we see the full splendid form. We hold the image, all feathers spread widely shining in silver, purple and white. The top of the crown-like wings hosts a beautiful eye. Innumerable eyes are wide-spread around the peacock, who greets us:

'Hello, peace be with you. Welcome to our blissful paradise. I am Padala.'

We smile. Smile and give thanks to the moment and Padala.

Padala says, 'come and explore the wide land on my back.'

We hop on and start our journey. Breathe and feel the lightness come with every breathing, in and out. With every breath we feel lighter and lighter, lifting up the sky above. 10 meters off the ground, 20 meters of the ground, 40 meters of the ground. We lift higher and higher with every breath we take. 100 meters of the ground, we can see the crowns of the trees, the peaks of the mountains and in the far, the endless horizon.

We fly in one direction and fly intensely. Breathe and breathe intensely. We are safe with Padala, so start to watch your breath again equally going in and out.

'I will bring you to my master, he lives in the paradise valley.'

We come to fly and see there is a vast green valley with a sacred stream and many abundant flowers and fruits. We come closer and closer, 100 meters, 80 meters, 40 meters, we breathe through and slowly get a feel of this paradise valley. A Lush and plentiful scent of the land makes us feel peaceful. 20, 10, 1 meter off the ground, we slowly descent with Padala down to the green valley field.

We sigh of relief and gasp for fresh air. The land smells nicely and we find the beautiful Padala walking us to a small little hut, where a shimmering light protects the entrance. Only you can come here with your companion and guide Padala. We open the door and in this little hut there sits a person, so familiar and wise, the face shines in a transcendental glow of joy and happiness. We recognize this face and observe a warm welcoming smile. We smile back and give thanks for the invite to the masters home.

'You have come a long way, take rest and come to ease. We will have tea soon.' The masters long white robe shimmers of purity and wisdom. We will hold the stillness and peace for a while so one can ask any question to the wise master.

(Holding silence)

We breathe and come out of the silence for another smile.

, Here', the master says, 'take this favourite feather and you will be welcome everywhere you go, just open it for the host to see.'

The master gives us a feather.

'This feather is a sign of peacefulness and lightness, keep it dear to your heart.'

We accept and bow in reverence.

We leave and come back to The Valley. We breathe and come back to our body, we sigh and come back to the room. Chant Om Shanti, Shanti, Shanti.

Frieden, Peace, Shalom.

Close your palms together, give thanks to the peacock Padala, the master and all living beings alike.

Meditation for Trust

Find a comfortable seat, bringing your whole body into balance between earth and sky. You can sit or lay on the ground in a comfortable place. Watch your breath coming equally in and out. Working with the breath is the one fundamental trust, as we live, we breathe.

Come to terms with your body, come to ease, settle, there is nothing to fear, relax, with a voice that is guiding you into meditation.

Just trust the breathing as it is coming and going, gently notice the breath and be aware of the sensation of the breath entering the nostrils and leaving them again.

Equally in and out again, breathe and be aware of how it comes into your nose tip, into your body and your heart.

Here in the heart, the breath is home. The beloved invites the lover and everything comes home. One can notice there is awareness in the breath which is bringing us home into the body and the heart.

We notice every part of the body, from the heart to the belly, to the spine, to the shoulders and head, and even to the tippy toes. Feel how the heart is opening and the chest is widening. Here in the heart is where the eternal spark of light resides.

Breathe out all you are letting go of and receive all you breathe in. One can make up a thought, we are letting go, and we can make up a thought that we receive, therefore we can inhale I Am Trust, and exhale all that we are not. Breathe, in I am Trust and breathe out again. Continue and know that the thought and words travel with the breath, into your heart.

Find peace and relax the body, coming to a state of trust and harmony.

With every single breath, one is becoming lighter and lighter. I am Light travels with the breath and comes into every cell of the body. The whole body is now very light and even so light it starts to float and lifting of the ground, just with the help of the breath.

The body is so light and trusting the body floats into the space of Trust, the whole body is now fully in a space of trust and peace. Feel the ease, the small breeze from the air entering the nose and coming to the heart.

In our imagination we can see a nice tender space where we can land again for good care, like in a flower field, full of moss and soft ground, landing there it feels like we are home in a space of trust and balance.

Feel the balance of the breath, equally inhaling and exhaling, as the thoughts arise we can just notice them like we notice the leaves dancing in the wind.

See the beautiful wind playing with the trees, also these trees are giving us shelter and equanimity, just trust and find a nice space close to that tree.

The trees are holding up the earth and likewise, we can hold trust within us, just steady and always growing up towards the sky.

Embrace nature and feel the rhythm of the breath, find the heart and maybe there is a friend who likes to join us.

Do you have a friend you like to play with? Invite this friend with a smile into the garden within the heart.

This friend is appearing with also a smile greeting us dearly and giving us a glance of gratitude and compassion. Trust is our friend and we have the happy community of someone who knows the way.
Let's sit and listen to the spring source that is coming down the stream, the subtle element makes us clear and the friend smiles again.

To trust means to have full faith in goodness.

Whatever will be, everything turns out just for a reason. Therefore always be thankful and happy for all the little things. Even watch the flowers who are so happily growing on the field providing nectar for the bees, and see the trees?
Do they ever complain? Still and steady they hold on for days and days on end, especially when there is a good friend. Walking along the small stream, the water is crystal clear and there is a fish or two within the river that flows into the lake of consciousness.
One can sit on the lake and watch the eagle birds glide and hover for good. Effortless the wind is holding them in space and every face is enjoying the fresh breeze, nothing better than this.

The eagle glides in a circular motion upwards without any flaps and the beauty of the moment seems to last forever, light and kind, the trust is in the air, who else should care?
There is the lovely friend, the family, or maybe the brother or sister and when everyone you know comes together, then it is time for a nice festivity.
On the lake, there is much to see, as some great mountains are erected on the vast horizon giving us a glimpse of majesty, the royal throne of the earth's surface, and up above there thrones the sun within the space.
All elements give a nice picture and the community plays music, or just enjoys the peaceful, trusting moment of harmony and whenever there is a light there can be equanimity.
Finding a reflection in the lake, one can see a mirror face of the wonderful surface, within this endless space.
Holding the moment of trust, even when there is no doubt, no lack and desire to be somewhere else, that is balance and trust.

Giving a hand to someone, and see there is a smile that illuminates the world, that is trust. Even together or just being alone, that is trust. Know to be content even when there is a surprising event, like a dancing tree.
Without any fault, everything finds a place on this earthly surface, even the rain. All come the same, yet we trust and have everything we need. A shelter is right there. But behold, there is a light within the hut, there might be someone in there. All in care, just trust and see, everything is in divine harmony.
'Knock, knock someone there?' The door opens and it is our favourite teacher, simply waving with a hand, smiling and inviting into his land. A shelter of hope and peace, just trust and feel the ease.
Warm and cosy it shall be, yes there is a certain equanimity. A stove heats the water for tea and the smell of wood is right with thee. How come we are also all living this dream collectively?
Life is miraculous and wonderful as sometimes unexplainably we just trust and see the magic unfold within the matter of the now, breathing and opening our hearts for the chance of goodness, one shall receive the mercy of the light.

' I have no fright, as I know it is forever and alright. Life as it is, the spirit shall go on and on.'
The tea boils and one can maybe feel a little of that spirit of life, being timeless and eternal, forever lasting like the connecting of the friends and family. Whatever shall be, shall be.
In the future we trust in Peace, Love and Unity, knowing everything is in divine harmony. Breathe equally. Notice the subtle sensation of the thoughts and the breath coming to terms with the light, knowing everything shall be alright. The perfect harmony is here, within the heart of everyone.
The flowers and the trees, the friends and families all together like to live in harmonies. All are the same in their goal to come back home.
Where the heart is there is bliss, and all longing to never miss a chance of meeting someone new, just trust and what we will do? Smile and breathe, greet as a friend always and forever one to be.
Then, all shall be happy.

Within the whole body, there is now the light of trust spreading and we can know that all living entities are seeking the same light of trust, and trust is everywhere and there and within the heart. Like there is air within the space there is love for all in the face of a smiling heart.
We are all a part of this world. Even when the sun sets for a goodbye it shall still shine, let's embrace the stillness of the lake one more time and see the setting suns face shining for a good night over the hills and within the heart, all we are a part.
This space is here and now for us to feel, from the tippy-toes to the head, to the chest and all around the nose, with the jaw and around the neck, the arms, shoulders and hands are relaxed, as well as the fingertips and the lips, the jaw and the neck.
The whole body is filled with lightness and trust, as we breathe there is no must, but we can do, whatever there is to do! We can also trust! Where there is no must, just let be, and feel free to also renounce and come back home to the premises of the body where the soul finds its heart.
There, everything is a start and we begin to breathe.

Be aware of the breath and let it flow naturally, just be aware of the body and relax from the head to the toes. The sunshine is now all gone, yet one can see the reflection within the sky, that is coming in beautiful colours and o 'wonder why we deserve to be blessed. Of course, because we trust.
Let's adjust the body to find a comfortable way, of trusting our close ones every day, maybe invite them for a dream with the heart-full space of trust, giving oneself to the best.
Give thanks and appreciation to the best ones close by, and be grateful for every single breath, as it comes naturally, we give thanks to nature accordingly.
All the appreciation to the world family.
May all beings be happy and live in equanimity.
Now, close the eyes and see yourself, just sitting in a nice tranquil state of equilibrium. This beautiful light of love surrounds you, and here you can take shelter, with all the joy and gratitude.
Maybe now, you can see yourself from head to toe, from toe to head, and again from head to toe. Nice light surrounds you and helps you to grow.

As the sun shines we all need light to grow, for a moment we can see our friends and family within this world. With light and growth. Smile and greet all the known faces.

Be aware again of the heart and be aware of the breath. This is your shelter, and only you know the truth within your heart, so does every person know the truth within their hearts.
Let the truth shine, and just relax, as a smooth chant can help purify and prepare for the night.
I am the Light of the World,
I am the Light of the World,
I am, I am, I am the Light of the World.
You are the Light of the World,
You are the Light of the World,
You are, you are, you are the Light of the World.
We are the Light of the World,
We are the Light of the World,
We are, we are, we are the Light of the World.
Be happy and smile

Imagine there is a light, a beautiful light, that shines from within
your heart. It is so bright and beautiful, it's around your whole body.
Breathe and feel the lightness throughout the whole body. See that light expanding with every breath. In and out, the breathing is equal and natural, the light expands and surrounds even the aura around you.
From within your heart there shines the source of this light and with every breath, we illuminate our whole body, from the head, one can see the head glowing in a beautiful protective light, to the feet. With every breath, the light travels throughout the body.
We start from the crown of our head, there is a light slowly sinking into the face. We breathe and with every breath, the light sinks lower and lower into the area of the eyes. Our eyes and all the muscles around the eyes are illuminated with protective, healing light.

Just focus on the breathing and let the light sink into the ears, the cheeks and the jaw. All the little tissues and membranes are equally illuminated, around the nose, on the jaw, and inside of the head, where the nose meets the mouth. We focus on this point, where the nose meets the mouth and sense our breathing. We can even hear the breath coming in and going out again. It is a constant stream of energy that comes with the air, and the sound is clear and soothing.
One can find comfort in the sound of the breath and know there is a light, a life protection from within and around us.
The Life Breath is everyone's mandatory need and we can connect with this friend our whole life. It is always there for us. Let's breathe again and feel how mandatory and friendly the life air is.

See the focus where the nose and mouth meet. and sense the air coming into the nostrils and going out again. It is a constant Hello, Breath. Goodbye Breath. Always and ever coming and going. We are just witnessing this process, this endless stream and ensure everything is smooth and equal.
Equally in and out again, the protective light shines within our whole head and a feeling of peace and protection spreads around the face. We can smile and ease into the breath. Maybe sigh or yawn, whatever feels now fine with you.
Also note any sensation, whatever it is, warmth, cold, vibrating, tickling, throbbing, pulsing, any sensation is possible, and whatever comes, we keep on breathing.

We see the breath travelling into our nostrils and down the throat into the lungs. From our head and our heart the protective light also illuminates the throat and neck area.

Along the spine, the protective light shines in every cell from the head, to the throat, to the middle of the body.

Here the light sinks further down with the breath and we include as many parts as possible, like the shoulders and arms, elbows, wrists and hands.

All are surrounded by protective light. We can open our hands to the sky and see how the light illuminates now every cell, even the fingertips.

Let's put our hands into our middle, onto the belly and feel into the body. Protective light is spreading from the hands and the heart into the belly and around the whole lower body.

The healing light of protection expands and brings peace and ease.
We breathe and with every breath, the light sinks further down the spine, from the belly to the hips, into the root of the spine.

Here we relax and find that the healing light of protection is welcome to also illuminate our thighs, knees, legs, ankles and feet. The healing light of protection even shines into the smallest parts of the tippy toes and brings peace and relaxation.

From the tippy toes we can come upwards, according to our breath we can travel with the awareness, the light of protection up the legs, to the bottom of the spine and again, slowly up the spine to the heart. Here, in the heart, we hold this healing light of protection and let it blossom like a flower.

With every breath, each pedal of this wonderful flower of light expands from the heart and shines throughout the whole body.

The whole flower of light is now really beautiful and blossoming. We can imagine we are meeting a friend, and we can bring this flower as a present to the heart of this friend.

Let's smile and innerly say: Here, this is the light of my heart, may it protect and bring you peace.

You can repeat this prayer and see your friend kindly accepting it.
Here, this is the flower of my heart, may it protect and bring you peace.
Here, this is the flower of my heart, may it protect and bring you peace.

Here, this is the flower of my heart, may it protect and bring you peace.

By saying this we give meaning to the flower and the light, therefore one knows what this light intends to do.

Protection and Peace is now upon us and we can see the whole body of ours and our friend be illuminated. By breathing we uphold the light, by breathing we maintain the luminosity.

Whenever we are in a hurry, we can also call this protective light and ask for a healing light of protection. Please Light, Protect me, and give me shelter of Peace.

The healing light is like the breathing always with us, when we are aware of it, it comes into presence.

In our imagination let's wander around our home and in the garden to maintain this healing light. Just breathe and feel the connection to the sunlight.
See how the light of protection and the sunlight are the same.
See the trees and the grass, and know all this is grown from the sunlight, one with the light of protection.

See the sky and the endless horizon and know, your inner voice can always call for the light of protection.

May All beings be in protection and Peace, May All find relaxation and ease.

May All have a life of light and love. May All live in Peace and Harmony, May All join the Unity.

This attractive light can bring us from the unsafe shores of darkness to the beautiful shores of the light kingdom.

Find yourself comfortable and relaxed, you are now safe and in protection.

Find a comfortable seat, bringing your whole body into balance between earth and sky. You can sit or lay on the ground in a comfortable place. Watch your breath coming equally in and out. Working with the breath is the one fundamental trust, as we live, we breathe.
Come to terms with your body, come to ease, settle, there is nothing to fear, relax, with a voice that is guiding you into meditation.
Just trust the breathing as it is coming and going, gently notice the breath and be aware of the sensation of the breath entering the nostrils and leaving them again.
Equally in and out again, breathe and be aware how it comes into your nose tip, into your body and into your heart.
Here in the heart the breath is home. The beloved invites the lover and everything comes home. One can notice there is awareness in the breath which is bringing us home into the body and into the heart.

 We notice every part of the body, from the heart to the belly, to the spine, to the shoulders and head, and even to the tippy toes. Feel how the heart is opening and chest is widening. Here in the heart is where the eternal spark of light resides.
Breathe out all you are letting go and receive all you breathe in. One can make up a thought, we are letting go, and we can make up a thought that we receive, therefore we can inhale I Am Trust, and exhale all that we are not. Breathe, in I am Trust and breathe out again. Continue on and know that the thought and words travel with the breath, into your heart.

Find peace and relax the body, coming to a state of trust and harmony.
With every single breath one is becoming lighter and lighter. I am Light travels with the breath and comes into every cell of the body. The whole body is now very light and even so light it starts to float and lifting of the ground, just with the help of the breath.
The body is so light and trusting the body floats into the space of Trust, the whole body is now fully in a space of trust and peace. Feel the ease, the small
breeze from the air entering the nose and coming to the heart.

In our imagination we can see a nice tender space where we can land again for good care, like in a flower field, full of moss and soft ground, landing there it feels like we are home in a space of trust and balance.

Feel the balance of the breath, equally inhaling and exhaling, as the thoughts arise we can just notice them like we notice the leaves dancing in the wind.
See the beautiful wind playing with the trees, also these trees are giving us shelter and equanimity, just trust and find a nice space close to that tree.
The trees are holding up the earth and likewise we can hold trust within us, just steady and always growing up towards the sky.
Embrace nature and feel the rhythm of the breath, find the heart and maybe there is a friend who likes to join us.
Do you have a friend you like to meet? Invite this friend with a smile into your light space of heart.

This friend is appearing with also a smile greeting us dearly and giving us a glance of gratitude and compassion. Trust is our friend and we have the happy community of someone who knows the value of life.

Let's sit and listen to the spring source that is coming down the stream, the subtle element makes us clear and the friend smiles again.

To trust means to have full faith in goodness in personality.

There is the lovely friend, the family, or maybe the brother or sister and when everyone you know comes together, than it is time for a nice festivity.
On the lake there is much to see, as some great mountains are erected on the vast horizon giving us a glimpse of majesty, the royal throne of the earths surface, and up above there thrones the sun within the space.

All elements give a nice picture and community plays music, or just enjoys the peaceful, trusting moment of harmony and whenever there is a light there can be equanimity.
Finding a reflection in the lake, one can see a mirror face of the wonderful surface, within this endless space.

Holding the moment of trust, even when there is no doubt, no lack and desire to be somewhere else, that is balance and trust.

Giving a hand to someone, and see there is a smile that illuminates the world, that is trust. Even together or just being alone, that is trust. Know to be content even when there is a surprising event, like a simple friend.

Without any fault everything finds a place on this earthly surface, even the rain. All come the same, yet we trust and have everything we need. A shelter is right there. But behold, there is a light within the hut, there might be someone in there. All in care, just trust and see, everything is in divine harmony.
'Notice the subtle sensation of the thoughts and the breath coming to terms with the light, knowing everything shall be alright. The perfect harmony is here, within the heart of everyone.
The flowers and the trees, the friends and families all together like to live in harmonies. All are the same in their goal to come back home.
Where the heart is there is bliss, and all longing to never miss a chance of meeting someone new, just trust and what we will do? Smile and breathe, greet as a friend always and forever one to be.
Then, all shall be happy.

Within the whole body there is now the light of trust spreading and we can know that all living entities are seeking the same light of trust, and trust is everywhere and there and within the heart. Like there is air within the space there is love for all in the face of a smiling heart.

We are all a part of this world. Even when the sun sets for a goodbye it shall still shine, let's embrace the stillness of the lake one more time and see the setting suns face shining for a good night over the hills and within the heart, all we are a part.
This space is here and now for us to feel, from the tippy-toes to the head, to the chest and all around the nose, with the jaw and around the neck, the arms, shoulders and hands are relaxed, as well as the finger tips and the lips, the jaw and the neck.
The whole body is filled with lightness and trust, as we breathe there is no must, but we can do, whatever there is to do! We can also trust! Where there is no must, just let be, and feel free to also renounce and come back home to the premises of the body where the soul finds its heart.
There, everything is a start and we begin to breathe.

Be aware of the breath and let it flow naturally, just be aware of the body and relax from the head to the toes. The sunshine is now all gone, yet one can see the reflection within the sky, that is coming in beautiful colours and o' wonder why we deserve to be blessed. Of course, because we trust.
Let's adjust the body to find a comfortable way, of trusting our close ones each and everyday, maybe invite them for a dream with the heart-full space of trust, giving oneself to the best.
Give thanks and appreciation to the best ones close by, and be grateful for every single breath, as it comes naturally, we give thanks to nature accordingly.

All the appreciation to the world family.
May all beings be happy and live in equanimity.
Now, close the eyes and see yourself, just sitting in a nice tranquil state of equilibrium. This beautiful light of love surrounds you, and here you can take shelter, with all the joy and gratitude.

Maybe now, you can see yourself from head to toe, from toe to head, and again from head to toe. Nice light surrounds you and helps you to grow.

As the sun shines we all need light to grow, for a moment we can see our friends and family within this world. With light and growth. Smile and greet all the known faces.
Be aware again of the heart and be aware of the breath. This is your shelter, and only you know the truth within your heart, so does every person know the truth within their hearts.
Let the truth shine, and just relax, as a smooth chant can help purify and prepare for the night.
I am the Light of the World,
I am the Light of the World,
I am, I am, I am the Light of the World.
You are the Light of the World,
You are the Light of the World,
You are, you are, you are the Light of the World.
We are the Light of the World,
We are the Light of the World,
We are, we are, we are the Light of the World.
Be happy and smile

Rest, relax and find shelter within eternity. Trust is with you.

Meditation for Patience

Peace and Patience, Trust and Surrender, everything shall turn out just fine. Equally breathe and be aware of the breath. Alive, and breathing. Gratefulness and appreciation are spreading across the horizon of hope and the sunlight of consciousness sets slowly but surely.

The sun always shines, even when the world spins its rounds, the sun doesn't give up shining the next moment. The moon does reflect, here and there and everywhere. Notice, it is just the perception of an individual that one perceives day, night, light and darkness according to the sky. Have you ever wondered why, this phenomenon of dark and light plays like it does?

If so, one can find a simple answer within the matter of the breath. Patiently and persistently, one can breathe, sun and moon, rise and fall, day and night, all dualities are also here to be found within the breath. In and out, are just states of consciousness that make all the matter move and groove. The interplay of elements is singular and dualistic at the same time, simultaneous oneness and difference. This simple truth is found within the sky. Yes, it is so simple, however it shines, it is shining not
only for one within this moment but for all. So, how can there be darkness, even though the sun is shining? Mysterious, isn't it?

The breath is like always present, so is energy. Light, energy and the universal life force or breath are always there and presently aware. Just inhale and find patience within these mystical questions of life.
We are also here to wait and receive answers, not to force. Let the answers of the universe come to you, and don't struggle with finding answers. Be constant and equanimous even if answers come to you. Be aware and happy, that one is breathing and alive, what a greater achievement and jive? Life is precious, protect it and keep it safe. Always watching it happening, right here and now.

Just appreciate and wait, bliss is present with us. Just keep steady and focus on the breathing and one is bound to be successful. With life there comes duality, this means happiness and distress, as well as light and dark, however, if one finds the transcendental truth behind all matter of duality, the curtain is lifted. The veil of Illusion can guide us and bring us a good show, but one has to humbly admit that this is not reality.

The truth means unity. The everlasting principle of the sun and moon means balance and unity. Only through unity of sun and moon, life on earth is possible. Same happens when man and woman come together, only through unity life is possible. The same happens within all elements, every moment and within every heart.

The spiritual heart actually only knows unity. Separation can become an intense longing for unity, but it is never the absolute truth. The Absolute Truth is a Person of all completeness and wholeness. Everything emanating from this Complete Whole is also perfect and complete, so is every breath, every moment, every single individual.

Be patient with oneself and see the eternal reality behind the things, emotions and words. There is likewise warmth and heat emanating from the sun, not just light. The light transforms into many varieties of forms and energies, but it remains one source.

And even the sun has a source. Why is this important? Because through yoga we learn unity and the complete wholeness, knowing there is one absolute source of all energies and matter.

Be patient, there are endless mysteries remaining, and none of this unnecessary business of trying to be rich, or famous, or popular is truly lasting, only the pure presence of being one with the truth can show one, how small and insignificant one really is. Breathe and notice how every single, yet so small breath, is important and making one live a life. Does the small and insignificant breath ever stop? No. It flows on and one experiences all life, just remember, next time you are waiting for a friend, or an enemy, just remember, that everyone is breathing the same air. The same life air is connecting all the beings. Every little creeper or even huge animals, humans and super humans, they all are dependent.

Breathe and notice the breathing refreshing one, sobering one and connecting one to all. Feel the breathing, naturally flowing and be patient, the truth is coming to light eventually.

Be patient, perfection is dawning, but next moment it can turn around and everything is changed. We all are the same in this regard. We are all on the same path, living a life, breathing and looking for happiness. We are all likewise differently searching. One uses yoga and meditation to come to eternal happiness, the other one needs a bed of flowers, the other one needs to dream big, and the other one needs to remember what is life and what is not.

Patiently and steadily one is on the path of self-awareness and realization. But first... let one breathe, the first conscious breath, full of bliss and happiness.
Are you remembering the first sight of the night sky? Or the first bonfire with the family? Maybe the first time on the ocean? Here is a meditative story for a journey to patience.

There once upon a time in a sweet village on the great ocean lived a family. Sometimes the sea was very mild, sometimes it was very harsh. According to the wind, the sound of the ocean could impress the whole family for a night or day. All were watching the majestic theatre of the waves coming and going again.

The breath likewise is coming and going, just like the waves of the sea.

The family joined for a walk together with the neighbour family and patience behold, waiting all for good, there shall be a night long of shooting stars.

So as the families waited the shooting stars came in and stardust illuminated the sky as the children and parents gazed in awe.

In the next moment there was not just one but many of the shooting stars. One of the Family members called out for this direction and another family called out for that direction. In all directions there were flashes of glittery, silver light up in the dark night.

Even though it was a little cold, it was worth the wait and wait patiently, there is more to see, the sea reflects the moon right into the night and the families share stories and tellings of all mysteries.

While the elders prepare a nice and warm fire place, one of the boys tells a story of Atlantis, a hidden gem of city far below the sea, where fish, shark, turtle, octopus and the Lord of the Sea Neptune live happily together.

The story goes on with the fire already set, beautiful and nice, the warmth of the sparkling flame illuminates the night. The stars are out and there we see a special meeting point of Saturn and Jupiter.

Saturn was a great hero who came to earth as a teacher, a wise person who saved the faithful people from the sunken continents.

Saturn is also so great because he has always a chakra, a wheel, with him and with this he protects the pious ones.

It is also a wheel of duty, as the wise teacher tells us what to do and what not to do, because Saturn has the great position in the sky.

Another Great position in the sky has Jupiter, the Greatest Star. Like any practice has mastery, the character of Jupiter is great perfection and joy.

With knowledge both of these planets can be seen during the night sky, especially on a nice clear night.

O and see, there is Venus, the romantic planet of Love. Called after the Goddess of Love, who also came to earth to enjoy the pleasure of being human, eating, relaxing and enjoying a nice fire.

Actually there is a planet for the fire element, and that is Mars who is named after a warrior. This planet is also visible with the mere eye, one just has to know where the planet is traveling.

Why do I tell you all this?

Because all these things are here with us, like sunshine and rain, like tides, like all in life, these heavenly friends have a character and they are here to illuminate us, and to give us balance.

When one is not feeling nice, then it is advised to pray to the Sun, and especially to the Sun-god.
'Please help me o dear Sun! I need your strength and light to be healthy and nice again.'

It really works. Other planets have other occupations but you can try to talk to all of them. Especially the moon is very responsive and kind.

With lots of patience these planets all come along and respond, with joy and gratitude one can also experience the wonderful earth.

Together the family sings some nice melodies and here the sound of the waves are giving a nice background, that enlivens the mood of everyone.

Cheer Up, be happy and sing, are we waiting for something?
Waiting, waiting, waiting the whole life to move, let's go and groove,
let's sing and dance,
let's enjoy the chance,
to be here together,
and maybe forever
there is the light,
even in the night.

These planets have been inhabiting the universe for years and years on end, it seems forever, yet they also eventually will find a home to stay.

Each moment, each and everyday,
one can embrace the wait and say;
Hey, what a bliss to be alive,
why the struggle and the strive,
let's be happy and sing,
peace within everything,
every heart in harmony,
Balance, Life is unity.

Just breathe and come to serenity. The stars will move, the sky will change, the sun may shine, yet the breath is personally thine.

Everyone connected like pearls on a string, now let's be happy and sing.
Whatever will be, will be.
The future is not ours to see, as it is, as it is.

Full of joy, happiness and bliss.

The family enjoys happiness and bliss together on the nice and warm fire place, straight on the ocean, the mild wind touches the face.

Can you feel the wind, the smooth breath on the nose tip, within the face?

Is there enough space, can we ask for more, all the life is here to adore.

Let's embrace the chance and unite the voice, with a simple song repeating just like that.

I am the Light of the World,
I am the Light of the World,
I am, I am, I am the Light of the World.

You are the Light of the World,
You are the Light of the World,
You are, You are, You are the Light of the World.

We are the Light of the World,
We are the Light of the World,
We are, We are, We are the Light of the World.

Just listen and repeat as often as possible.
These words carry light, hope and happiness, they can vibrate with the light within the heart and there it shines forever and eternal.

Can we wait for eternity?

The wise one knows, only the eternal soul can, but who is to know something beyond the sky?

The community of friends and family looks into the sky, somethings are still for us to wonder, what leaves space, is the heavenly face, that makes us feel so small, but we can listen to the call, of patience and peace, like the desire trees.

Imagine sitting under a tree, full of compassion that provides thee with all you need. That is a desire tree, and are they for free, in the spiritual sky, beyond our life, within the heart of everyone.

Just breathe and be aware of the most subtle sensations of the breath and keep the breathing equal, in and out, equal, all the time.

The heart may be fulfilled with light, and so a simple smile shines bright. Just let it be, and there shall blossom peace and harmony.

Now, close the eyes and see yourself, just sitting in a nice tranquil state of equilibrium. This beautiful light of love surrounds you, and here you can take shelter, with all the joy and gratitude.

Maybe now, you can see yourself from head to toe, from toe to head, and again from head to toe. Nice light surrounds you and helps you to grow.

As the sun shines we all need light to grow, for a moment we can see our friends and family within this world. With light and growth. Smile and greet all the known faces.

Be aware again of the heart and be aware of the breath. This is your shelter, and only you know the truth within your heart, so does every person know the truth within their hearts.

Let the truth shine, and just relax, as a smooth chant can help purify and prepare for the night.

I am the Light of the World,
I am the Light of the World,
I am, I am, I am the Light of the World.

You are the Light of the World,
You are the Light of the World,
You are, you are, you are the Light of the World.

We are the Light of the World,
We are the Light of the World,
We are, we are, we are the Light of the World.

Be happy.

Rest, relax and find shelter within eternity. Patience is the key.

The matter of breathing has a wonderful duality, referring to the masculine and feminine aspect of nature. This nature is also linked up with the sun and the moon, and all other stars are included. The masculine aspect of the king of all planets, the sun, is most likely comparable with a royal king who holds all the wealth and power within his realm, always focused and beaming light into all directions the sun gives life and destruction equally.

It is the whole spectrum of power and life. It is the whole spectrum of light.

The moon in this regards is the feminine counterpart and only what the sun can give to receive, the moon can reflect unto the little planet earth who is secretly living due to perfect balance.

Patiently and persistently all these protagonists are floating, dancing and rotating in outer space, just by the grace of the Supreme Balance that holds everything in personal harmony.

Sometimes demons come and throw the earth into the waters of ignorance but the Supreme Personality rescues the eart again and again, because it is very dear to the Complete Balance in Person.

Thus one can appreciate the life that is present and prospering, only by the mercy, grace and blessings of the Supreme Overseer who protects the earth.

Patiently existing, life is so vast and grant, calculations have measured that the whole existence is created through one breath of the Creator, who then inhales for once. Spanning many hundreds of trillions of years, the breathing takes place, and just through one exhalation the whole manifestation is vanquished again.

This is depicted in sacred scriptures like the Srimad Bhagavatam.

Just breath and feel into the belly, here patience and creative force reside. Be humble and tolerant like a tree, giving many fruits of wisdom, enlightening the hearts of all beings. Just breathe to check, how fast you breathe and lean back, to breathe slower. Lean forward to breath quicker, quenching the belly like a lemon, the breathing can be altered but just hold one hand on the heart, and one shall know, what is the proper, individual breathing rats. It is as unique as ones voice.

Patiently chant:

I am the Patience in this World,
I am eternal within this World,
I am, I am, I am eternal patience in this world.

You are Patience in this World,
You are eternal within this World,
You are, You are, You are eternal patience in this World.

We are Patience in this World,
We are eternal within this World,
We are, We are, We are eternal patience in this World.

Just breathe and feel into your heart, notice the internal play of all elements, and just be aware of life, as it is.

Meditate, chant and be happy.

Meditation for Self-Awareness and Preservation

Be aware and sit in a balanced position, so that the spine is erect and straight. Proper sitting is half the deal, if one finds a perfect seat, life, breathing and meditation becomes easier and lighter.

The seat must be neither to high nor too low, and one shall adjust oneself towards the North, meditating facing North is beneficial and gives a better experience. Facing North, it is said in scriptures, the wise sages and moon are addressed. Give it a sit, and breathe equally.

Breathing for self-awareness means breathing for wisdom of body, mind and self. First one starts to be aware of the breathing, coming equally in and out again, then one can be aware of the heart and heart beat, rhythmic and steady. From here, one can be aware of the belly, and tongue. Both play a crucial role in self control.

Put the tongue towards to roof of the mouth and just put one hand on the navel, feeling the breathing. Also, it is best, to let the breathing be equal, by inhaling the belly is rising, by exhaling, the belly is deflating. In and out are equal, and the belly moves with the breath. Inhale, belly rising, exhaling, belly deflating. Practice makes perfect and equal breathing can be beneficial in any life situation.

While breathing notice the spine being erect and in balance. The buttocks shall be firmly on the mat, or Meditation seat. The neck and shoulders shall be relaxed and flexible. Soft eyes and muscles around the scalp make it easy to witness the sensations. One can be aware that there is a consciousness behind the body that controls and maintains it. Without this consciousness the body is just a sac of blood, amino-acids, and bones. The real life happens in consciousness, which travels with the breath.

The breath is the fine string which connects the body, mind and soul. It is the means to also control mind and body. However difficult, mind and body can be equally still and present, as a perfect transportation through life.

Imagine a carriage pulled by five horses, and led by one driver. Within this carriage transportation there is a dormant personality sitting within, slumbering and dreaming away.

The five horses are the senses, namely, smell, taste, sight, touch and hearing, according to the sense organs nose, tongue, eyes, skin and ears. In accordance to the fundamental elements of earth, water, fire, air and ether.

The one leading the carriage is the intellect having the slings of the mind within his hand. The intellect is steadily directing the ride, keeping the carriage on track. In the back, slumbering and dreaming away, that is the soul, or personification of consciousness.

This personality is trusting in the abilities of the expert driver, the intellect, who directs the steps, with the mind, of all the horses.
The carriage, representing the body, is pulled then on this track called life.

Sense attraction is the biggest obstacle on the spiritual path, and in meditation, because the senses are so fine, especially hearing, they are easily misdirected. Though even finer, the mind and intellect have to control so that life is in balance. Henceforth, the personality or Self can be brought easily to the desired goal.

The Self is conscious only when it is purely align with the spiritual nature of things. Consciousness is the expression of this Self, and hence forth it is the finest of all material elements, it pervades everything and helps one to be alive, through the matter of breath.

Concluding, the breath is the connection of body, mind and soul. The soul, or Self, is conscious, even of mind, body and senses, when one is aware of the breath being everywhere.

Breath, or the element of sky pervades everything, even matter, bones, blood, and skin. Therefore, one can be aware of ones own tippy toe, just by breathing, and consciously being aware of oneself.

Now, let us make a journey, along the matters of body, to the whole body. This can serve as a relaxation and is also meant to give protection and preservation, because where there is consciousness, awareness and the life force of the breath, there is life.

Life means awareness, therefore it is a win-win for everyone. One just has to trust, that there is an infinite source of awareness within the living beings heart, that is all.

Just trust, and see the breath constantly flowing. Be present and aware. Notice the scalp, the muscles around the head and the jaw. Be aware of the head. Fully, breathe in and out. Let go and relax the jaw, neck and muscles of the shoulders. There is a crucial point of relief behind the ear flap. Get two fingers and stroke it nicely, from behind the ear flaps to the chin, on both sides, and sigh.

Put the fingers on the temples and circulate. Let the temples and muscles around the eyes be relaxed and relieved, but most importantly, be aware of such areas. Be aware and relax.

Be aware of the shoulders, arms, elbows, wrists and hands, even so the fingertips and palms. Be aware and relax.

With awareness there comes natural balance. Relax and let it be. Balance is the status quo of nature. The body is nature, but in a certain way it has forgotten simple truths like the one of equality. See that everything is align. Alignment means in one perfect line vertical between sky and earth, and horizontal with the horizon. This is geometry of the body. Keep it simple and breathe. Even chant, and by doing so one let's nature act. This brings natural balance back.

Let Balance be, with awareness and happiness. Natural balance is also friendly and mindful. A smile conveys this message perfectly. Smile and charm yourself with this sunlight from the lips of one's living example of happiness. Be aware of the inner source of happiness and let it take over. This brings natural balance and happiness easily, into every situation.

Smiling gives relief, also to the jaw, shoulders and neck. It is the perfect antidote for all weakness of the body. Practice smiling within the mind, envision a big, bright and beautiful smile, as shiny as one rainbow and beautiful as a double-rainbow. Be that shiny lamp of happiness within the rainy season of grief and misery. Be happy and shine equally with body, mind and words.

Utter nice words that come to mind. Let the mind be as clean and beautiful as a clear lake. The words will be sweet mellows coming from this nice mind. The mind, it is said, once controlled, can be your best friend. However, if one is unable to have proper self-control and awareness, the mind takes over and plays hide-and-seek.

Things disappear, sometimes even oppose one, why? Because the mind is not align, and one is still looking for the true way of mindfulness. Smiling is one, meditation is another one, Mantra Meditation is probably the best one.

Chant and be happy, this helps to still the mind.

Chant:

I am the Light of the World,
I am the Light of the World,
I am, I am, I am the Light of the World.

You are the Light of the World,
You are the Light of the World,
You are, You are, You are the Light of the World.

We are the Light of the World,
We are the Light of the World,
We are, We are, We are the Light of the World.

Chant and repeat, or chant the Maha-Mantra for sublime, transcendental connections to the Supreme Personality Krsna.

Hare Krishna
Hare Krishna
Krishna Krishna
Hare Hare
Hare Rama

Hare Rama
Rama Rama
Hare Hare

This is the great chant for deliverance and thus one can attain control over the mind and senses, along with a straight connection to the Self.

Lord Krsna says in the Bhagavād-Gita:
'I am seated as Supersoul within everyone's heart.'
So this Supreme Personality is within everyone as the Superself or collective consciousness which connects all beings. This is a sublime truth.

With every word we utter, one can have impact on the world. Even a small word can sometimes alter the outcome of a result or even change a world matter. This has been proven by many examples in history, and by controlled breathing and chanting one can be super conscious of ones own words, mind and actions.

Breathing consciously can also be a great protection and preserver. Some yogis who live meditation are getting older than the norm, just by controlled breathing, and even modern yoga teachers, masters and practitioners recommend the process of prolonged and conscious breathing for balance, longevity and health.

This is wonderful, because it helps everyone. Likewise, everyone can learn it, and do it. It is easy. Just follow along.

Breathe equally in, feel the heart, and equally out again. Feel again. Breathe equally in, feel, and equally out again. Let the breath flow naturally and don't force anything, however for control one needs to apply conscious strength. One must be willing to.

Breathe in, and be aware of the subtle nature of the breath, holding it for once, and releasing it, naturally flowing out. Breathe in again, and let it naturally flow.

The small pause in-between in and out-breath is called kumbhaka and it is a true spiritual bridge, allowing one to be aware in stillness.

It is the perfect link to connect material and spiritual realms, from the in and out, to the out and in-breath. This minute pause, can be held, and therefore the breathing can be consciously controlled.

Some yogis hold this kumbhaka constantly and stop the process of breathing, to remain in Trance. This is not recommended and it needs proper guidance, to remain in balance.

It is much like riding a bicycle for the first time, with help of a cycle and teacher, one can ride, by oneself, riding is difficult. One also needs balance and steady practice to be able to do so. Same with the proper prolonged breathing. BKS Iyengar is an expert teacher who can deepen the practice, but for now, let's use the subtle light force to be light and alive.

The body is now relaxed and in a certain state of equilibrium, perfect. Now, come to terms with the balance of the mind. Be equally and consciously breathing rhythmically; In, one, two, three, four, and out again, one, two, three, four, one can practice the balance of mind and body.

We have also learned that the Mantra is highly effective for using the subtle link of consciousness to reach every part of the body.

I am Light means, that everything is pervades by consciousness, or the light of awareness. Thus, one can be fully aware. This light can also be protective light, light that is aware of fear, danger or calamities. Light has intelligence and whatever dawns, the intellect already knows what is behind the next corner, always.

This also includes sensing vibrations of fear, anxiety or danger. Calamities arise naturally, but one can have a feel for it. Knowing to be safe and sound, when something happens. This awareness arises from intuition and everyone has one. Ones intuition is sometimes called the sixth sense, which includes the mind. To be mindful means to use ones intuition properly to be guided by light, awareness and higher consciousness. It is intelligent to do so.

One shall be wise to use such protective light, to stay on the safe side, and also there are many prayers, stories and Affirmations for Protection. Here a little taste;

Just sit comfortably and witness the breathing coming in and out, be aware of the subtle sensations of the life air which is transferred to the heart. Here it is transformed into life force or prana, the subtle current of energy that makes the universe move.

By controlled breathing or pranayama, one can attract consciousness, through focus and determination one can deliberately open the gates of consciousness to set forth a river of energy. This source of this river and lake of emerging conscious energy or prana is the Supreme Origin, the source of all attraction.

See the Supreme Abundance sitting with very beautiful garlands and silks sitting on the patio, along with many servants and playmates. Some musicians recite beautiful verses and there is one who is constantly fanning the Supreme Person who sits comfortably on a throne of finest gold and jewels.

Within the moment the Supreme Personality is fully satisfied and so shall we be. Be aware, and happy to be alive. It is a blessing and a gift to live and have control over one's actions. Be aware of little sensations. Sit very comfortably and notice the body, full of awareness and in balance. The breathing goes in and out, equally, inhale and exhale hold a little gap in-between. Just notice the length of the inhale, be aware of the gap, then exhale and notice the length of the exhalation. Start all over and balance in and exhale, so they are of equal strength and length.

Don't force, let every breath flow naturally and consciously. Let the spine be erect and the chest wide and in harmony with the upper and lower body. Proper sitting is the means of perfect meditation. Cross-legged in the lotus posture is the prime of all Meditation positions, but meditation can work everywhere and with everyone.

Just sit comfortably and notice the buttocks on the ground, feel the spine erecting and straightening up, until one reaches the head where skull, jaw and neck are in alignment. The shoulders are relaxed. The muscles around the eyes are soft, if not, and this happens in daily life, one can massage the skin and muscles around the eyes. Rotate the eyes clockwise and shift your gaze from left to right, up and down. Circle again. This serves as a calibration of the gaze which is highly important.

This gaze shall be straight with an equanimous mind. Leave the eyes half open and half closed, be aware of the gaze naturally shifting towards the inner eye, the space between the eyebrows. Naturally, one can perceive an inner vision of the Supreme Balance, the origin of all consciousness. Here, one might also see a lake that is still and pure, that is the lake of consciousness. From this lake, all energies flow into life, and whatever gate, or doorway we open, the energy flows into this channel. This is how attraction finds a path of expression. This is how conscious energy becomes manifest.

One has to know what gate or doorway to open.

For now, be guided and aware of the gates of protection opening. The gatekeeper, a servant of the Supreme Balance, unlocks the power of will and sets free a stream of energy into the channel of protection. Protection is a simple and effective energy that surrounds us since time immemorial. Humans have sought shelter and protection wherever in history, and now we can imagine a great forest grove of ancient sequoia trees, the giant mammoth trees of the World, spanning a life of over 2500 years.

Hereunder such a tree, one can find an imaginative shelter and protection. The tree is very humble and wise to give shelter and so it has been the mercy of the forest grove to shelter us for this moment.

Breathe equally in and out, and be aware of the subtle nature of the forest. Strong and mighty these trees give confidence and patience, protection and peace. Just reciprocate and receive the eternal service of nature here on earth. With great trunks and huge energetic branches, the balance is upheld and energy can flow easily in these channels.

Be conscious and know that the Supreme Origin is also the source and seed of all energies, trees, forest and winds.
Be aware of the life air, fresh and serene flowing from the forest groves into the heart. The heartbeat is noticeably slower and finer, the air cleanses the energy channels and the purity of the forest gives protection to all impurities.

Honour and respect this magnificent place, and strength, protection and peace shall be present immediately.

Trees have been sheltering humans forever and still give presence, balance and protection. Whenever there is no way out, in daily life or meditation, just think about the forest and take (an imaginative) stroll around the groves of ancient forests. Be aware of the sounds, smells and presently, be aware of the heartbeat. Feel the tranquillity and shelter.

Trees are the great guardians of this earth and we have been guest for long enough to know that the elements are our friends. Likewise, the waters, which are gently flowing along the groves to nurture the land and animals. This beautiful place also holds flowers and herbs which are aromatic and lushly spread across the grove.

Breathe, and be aware that finding shelter is necessary, one can submit and see that life is always depending. The trees are creating the oxygen we need, and the other way around, the trees are absorbing the carbon dioxide of our lungs to transform it into oxygen. Naturally, the trees have been feeding us with oxygen, since life existed, and one can be eternally thankful.

Give thanks and appreciation to the forest grove, where a beautiful river flows, and where birds are singing a sweet song.

I am the Maintainer of the World
I am the Maintainer of the World
I am, I am, I am the Maintainer of the World.

You are the Preserver of the World,
You are the Preserver of the World,
You are, You are, You are the Preserver of the World.

We are the Sustainer of the World,
We are the Sustainer of the World,
We are, We are, We are the Sustainer of the World.

Just be humble and steady as a tree and life will flower.

Once upon a time, there lived the oldest and wisest trees in the world. These trees were so rooted, that no one could shake them, as these trees were holding onto the ground, no one could ever rip them out, no giant, no dragon, no king, nor queen, but they all know, the wonderful humbleness of a tree.
So humble and kind, the tree doesn't care, about all this, the tree is not winning any prize, but the honour and respect of all humankind. Even the wind, sometimes tries, but hardly comes to terms with this forest kingdom, where the trees hold onto their roots.

So find a comfortable position and imagine your spine. You see the spine, vertebrae for vertebrae and there is also a root, imagine, the root coming from the lowest bottom of the spine and spreading throughout the soil, into the layers of the ground. That ground then is the fundament for our balance.
So we breathe and breathe in the balance. Equally in and out, Balanced breath, equally in and out.

All in harmony and balance, the breathing flows naturally and the body is aligned with all the elements. As the spine is straight, we are relaxing our jaw and head. We can let go of any tension, to relax and ease, into a smile.

Breathe and smile, gently.
Breathe and be in balance.
Like the roots of a tree, we find steadiness in the ground.
And we can also tone a sound, that helps us to relax.

Let's open our mouth, wide and full, on AHHH, hold the sound as long as possible. AHHHH
Now breathe again and find the balance and harmony, in the ground, and of course, we can tone another sound.

This time for our heart, the Sound goes UHHHH, very mild and long, we can tone this once more, UUHHHH and there you connect to your heart and now let's embrace the smile, let's connect to our head with HUMMMM, long and gently, sound HUMMMMM. These three sounds, AHHH, UHHH, HUMMM are the essential building blocks of life.

Like a tree has a seed, that's the AAH, it also has a stem, that's the UHH, and of course, it has a crown and that's the HUMMM. All together these three sounds AUM give the primal sound, a wonderful attraction.

Sometimes, a lot of flowers are coming from a tree, sometimes, the tree dances in the wind to find expression, and sometimes the fruits of a tree are growing from just a little seed.

One seed has all the information a tree needs to live on for thousands of years, and even in the nights, the trees are growing upwards and downwards, isn't that interesting?
As all the beings, like the trees, are part of this world, we are also growing in the night, yet, we have to be sure, that we are relaxed and ready for the upcoming night. Therefore the trees prepared a nice soothing song for the upcoming good night.
It is again, around that time, where everything sets, from the shine, of the sun, to the son, of a kingdom divine. Please, enjoy the moment, and breathe, like we are here together to live.

Enjoy the moment and breathe, The air comes in and out, there is so much doubt,
But leave it all behind,
Be sure and one shall find,
That there is more to the dark,
That there is always a spark,

That ignites the wisdom of life.
Even though we respect the light,
We know, it must be night, Whenever we are in sight,
we arrange to be alright,
With a song, that goes all night long.
Sing it and feel it in the breath.
Sing it and feel it in the air,
Breathe and be enjoying the now. Everything is in care, just trust, just trust. There is no more, do's or must.

Just relax and keep the breath, Feel the peace and the ease.

Root yourself to the ground,
And hear the beautiful sound.
It is the air, in the space,
Now imagine a face,
Let it be kind and smile,
Hold it on for a while,
Enjoy the sight,
attracting the night

A moment we listen to the trees, we are also listening to our selves, conscious and wise, we are all rooted on the same earth.
Be kind and bring your friends, to this wonderful kingdom of peace and harmony. Enjoy every bit of it.

Meditation for Abundance & Satisfaction

Be in balance. Body and mind, breathe in and out. Equally in, equally out. Let there be space with every breath. Let there be freedom with every in & exhalation. Let it flow, like the abundant river we know. The source comes from within. Endlessly, tirelessly. Springing from the Self-fulfilment comes naturally. Peace, Love & Harmony all come naturally from within. Breathe. Equally in and out. See and observe your whole body.
From the core, a beautiful golden light fulfils your inner space. From the very core to the inner dimension and layers of all you are. Layer by layer every part of your body is flooded with shining golden light. From the core spreading to the skin, from the head to the toes. The whole body is illuminated with a beautiful golden glow fulfilling all there is. Now, Peace, Love and Harmony is with you. Now joy flows through every vein. Now satisfaction may be with you, too. Flowing through every part of your body. From Toe to Head and along the spine. Including your Back, including the heart, back to the head, to the face and the nostrils. Focus on the part below the nostrils, and observe the natural flow coming and going. Be aware of the natural breath. The natural flow of respiration. Observe that stream and see it coming in and going out. Equally in an equally out. Balance yourself and feel equanimity. Relax and rest.

Abundant Contentment

Just breathe. Observe and watch the natural breath as it is. Be aware of every sensation and know the balance within you. Feel the balance and equanimity within. Breathe equally in, equally out.

We see ourselves sitting in peace, right here, right now. See yourself in every situation that hosts contentment. May it be on a walk through your favourite part of the world. May it be a nice conversation with a loved one. May it be a chance to be in absolute serenity. Whatever it is, see yourself content, fulfilled and at peace. Rest in that image for a while and observe your breathing. Be aware of the sensation of the breath moving in and out, be aware of the image of yourself in contentment. Find yourself in total peace and reflect upon this image. May it be always there with you, whenever you come out of balance, come back to your natural breath and come back to that image of contentment. See yourself, observe yourself, rest in that peacefulness. See yourself within the moment of absolute peace and feel the peace. Just sitting there and breathing. Just being content and at peace.

Bring this image into your daily life, into the natural flow of your day. Include this image of yourself into the rhythm of your way. See how you nurture your inner peace and internal contentment. See yourself within daily life and see yourself content. Simply breathe. Equally in an equally out. Balance yourself and know the natural flow of life as it is. Relax and rest.

Start again. Breathe in and Breathe out. Watch the Flow and Feel the Sensation of the natural breath. If you cannot feel, slightly hard breathe intentionally and let it flow again. Watch the flow and feel satisfaction. One is Alive with the Breath. No breath, no life. Breathe and be at ease. Gently smile. Every Breath is another try for a good life. Make every breath count and be aware of the sensations.

Whatever comes, goes. All we fail, all the misery may come and go.

All the goodwill may come and go.

We are not perfect, we are still learning. Remind yourself of great dissatisfaction and remember to forgive yourself. Forgive and Receive the power to try again. Now Breathe in, Breathe out. Breathe satisfaction and forgiveness. Repeat for a while. Feel content and start again, try with a new insight and resolution. Dissolve with forgiveness, nurture with joy. Breathe joy, let go and forgive. Breathe in satisfaction and breathe out forgiveness. Now, remember yourself, with a second chance, to better, to come out of misery and failure, with goodwill. We are not perfect, but we can try our best.

Just see yourself as you are. See yourself as you are. Breathe in and out, equally in and equally out. Just feel. Bring your palms together and bow.

Observing joy in the world

Start to observe. The whole world in your breath. All the life that breathes is alive. Even the small pieces and parcels, even the plants and trees, even the bees and butterflies, even the animals, humans, all beings alike. All breathing, all alive. Just breathe, be with joy, breathe out. Let it flow. See yourself in a joyful glow of shining golden light. With every breathing expanding. Expand your light from the inside out, from the core to the universe. Breathe. Joy travels with the breath, so see all the beings with this golden light of joy, even in the smallest particle, see the light boundlessly expanding into the world, into the universe. Meet the sun, joyfully shining the light onto the world. See all the world connected to that light and observe yourself in this joyful light. Breathe into this light and be aware of every sensation. Be aware of the natural flow of the breathing. In and out. Every breath connects us to the world, to every being. All the joy is with us, glowing in a beautiful golden light. See the sun, see the joy, observe yourself and be aware of the balanced breath. In and out, observe, equally in and out. See your family, watch them happily be. Set yourself free and smile. With all the joy, all the happiness. May all the joy and happiness surround me.

Breathe. Enjoy.

May all the Joy surround me.

Palms together, in front of the chest, let the thumbs touch the heart. May all the joy surround me. Bow.

Cultivating joy

Be aware of your natural flow of respiration. The natural breath. Life. Coming in and going out. Whatever comes, it goes. Even love and joy, come and go. Breathe all the joy, let it flow out into the world. See all the beings within a golden light of joy. Let this golden stream be and find the joy inside. What is making me joyful now? What brings me lasting joy? Finding the core, finding the peace and harmony. First we still the mind by breathing. Joy, with the matter of happiness and lightness coming from that source. Stillness. Awareness. Happiness. Breathing in, stillness comes, breathing out, restlessness goes. Ease in and naturally breathe. Let it flow. Let all the joy come and let it go. Thoughts may come, thoughts may go. Keep a balanced mind and find joy within this equanimity. Find peace and harmony from the ease of breathing. Life is there. Breath opens the gates to joy. See it open and observe the joy as it is. Observe and be aware of the natural flow. Feel it sinking in, into the heart, into the root. Now breathe deeply into the root, into the ground, to cultivate to nature the soil of joy. Breathe with all the attention and love. See your breathing moving to the root, feel the bottom of the belly and be aware of the heart. Silence yourself. Rest.

Cultivating satisfaction

Connecting with the feeling of fulfilment and contentment that does exist within you

Breathe through. Like a big sigh, a relief, a liberation. A sigh of freedom. Imagine yourself on the peak of a mountain, totally liberated and free. Breathe the fresh air of fulfilment and be. Content you sit there and just breathe. See yourself just right there on the top, breathing and satisfied. Nothing to do, endless possibility. Just be and feel. Content and fulfilled. At peace. Just breathe. Bring your awareness to the natural flow of respiration and breathe every moment full of satisfaction. See yourself grow a smile of contentment and feel a sensation of peace. Breathe. Equally in and out. By breathing a feeling we cultivate the feeling. Within every cell of the body, feel the contentment and satisfaction. All the body is at peace. From the head to the feet. From feet to head.

Breathe and let the satisfaction wander along the body. From the head along the spine to the bottom, below to the feet. Let the feeling of contentment wander from the feet to the thighs to the buttocks. Along the spine up to the chest area, to the shoulders and neck. All fulfilled, all satisfied, flowing to the very peak of the head and the face. We breathe and create space. With every breathing satisfaction comes and goes. We keep the natural flow. Balance yourself. Relax

Joyful affirmations

This is a mantra meditation. The joyful affirmations can be repeated silently in your head or spoken out loud. Try to connect with the meaning behind the words.

May All the Joy be with All
May all the love be with all
May all the happiness be with all Love, Peace & Harmony
May all the Joy be with Us
May all the love be with Us
May all the happiness be with us. Love, Peace & Harmony
May all the Joy be with You
May all the Love be with you
May all the happiness be with you Love, Peace & Harmony
May all the Joy be with me
May all the love be with me
May all the happiness be with me Love, Peace & Harmony
I am the Joy of the World
I am the joy of the world
I am I am the joy of the world
You are the joy of the world You are the joy of the world

You are, you are, you are the joy of the world
We are the joy of the world
We are the joy of the world
We are, we are, we are, the joy of the world.
Love, Joy and Harmony Peace in Unity Satisfaction
Love Attraction
Joy and Harmony, Peace in Unity Satisfaction

Affirmations to attract life satisfaction

This meditation takes the form of a mantra. You can repeat the affirmations silently inside your mind or out loud if you prefer. Allow yourself to really feel the words and let them resonate.
Repeat each fresh phrase like a Kirtan, call and response.
I am satisfied with all there is, Nothing more, nothing less, Balance in equanimity,
Feel Peace and Harmony.
I am satisfied with you, Content and true, Here and Now,
I take a bow
Silence in my mind, Love in my heart,
We are all a part
Of a wonder world, From the breath, From east to the west, I Live to try the best.
I affirm to be content Here and Now,

With All there is
On the way to bliss,
I bow, Balance is now

Silence in my mind, Love in my heart,
We are all a part,
Of this moment world, A Moment to Moment, Breathe and feel, Peace, Love and Unity I affirm Harmony
Within all there is,
I am bliss,
I am Balance,
I am equanimity,
Peace, love and unity.
I meditate upon the Wholeness,
Balance for everyone,
Peace for everyone,
Love for everyone,
Unity for everyone,
Harmony for everyone,
Bliss for everyone
I meditate upon the Highest Absolute, May you be merciful with Us,
May we serve for the highest good of all, May we All live in Peace and Harmony. Love and Unity,
Here and Now,
I bow.
Namaste

Guided Meditations & Breathwork For Anxiety & Deep Sleep:

10+ Hours Of Affirmations, Hypnosis & Guided Breathing For Relaxation, Self-Love, Insomnia, Positive Thinking & Depression

© Copyright 2021 - All rights reserved.

The content contained within this book may not be reproduced, duplicated or transmitted without direct written permission from the author or the publisher.
Under no circumstances will any blame or legal responsibility be held against the publisher, or author, for any damages, reparation, or monetary loss due to the information contained within this book; either directly or indirectly.

Legal Notice:
This book is copyright protected. This book is only for personal use. You cannot amend, distribute, sell, use, quote or paraphrase any part, or the content within this book, without the consent of the author or publisher.

Disclaimer Notice:
Please note the information contained within this document is for educational and entertainment purposes only. All effort has been executed to present accurate, up to date, and reliable, complete information. No warranties of any kind are declared or implied. Readers acknowledge that the author is not engaging in the rendering of legal, financial, medical or professional advice.

Guided Meditations:

Breathwork: 89

Meditations for Anxiety 94

Meditation for Deep Sleep: 100

Affirmations: 120

Guided Breathing For: Relaxation 132

Self-Love 136

Insomnia 140

Depression & Positive Thinking 148

Breathwork:

This serves as introduction to all the meditations in the following.

Breathwork or conscious breathing is the method by which one can still the mind and the senses. When the senses, like tongue, eyes, ears, touch and voice are pacified, then a higher intelligence can sprout. By this a subtle seed is sown into the garden of the elements, namely earth, water, fire (light), air and ether. The whole cosmic manifestation, that which is present and perceive-able is composed of these elements. By stilling and equalizing the breath one links up the subtle realm of ether, mind, intelligence and ego with the realm of gross elements such as earth, water, fire and air. The life air is the means to balance all elements. Due to the subtle nature of the sky air can roam freely, but it always remains within the boundaries of the sky.

Through all elements pervades consciousness, but it is said in yogic scriptures that this most subtle and all-pervading element of consciousness travels with the breath. The life air, prana or breath, is the vehicle for the personality of consciousness. This consciousness has a wonderful character. It is never produced, nor destroyed, it is ever constant and immoveable. At the same time it makes all the movement possible. For example, are you aware of the subtle heart beat? Are you noticing the toes? Is there life, is there awareness, is there consciousness.

Conscious breathing and Breathwork plays together with proper posture, sitting, moving and standing. There it is recommended to find a common ground. The common ground should be a safe space to meditate where on can sit in proper peace and balance. It is recommended to create a room specifically for meditation so this magnificent practice can unfold its full potential.

It is recommend in the Vedic injunctions to prepare a meditation place as follows:

'To practice (yoga) meditation, one should go to a serene & peaceful place, one should lay kusa grass on the ground and then cover it with a skin or a soft cloth. The seat should be neither too high nor too low and should be situated in a sacred space. The meditator should then sit on it very firmly and practice yoga to purify the heart by controlling his mind, senses and activities and fixing the mind on one point.

One should hold one's body, neck and head erect in a straight line and stare steadily at the tip of the nose. Thus, with an unagitated, subdued mind, devoid of fear, completely free from sex life, one should meditate upon Me within the Heart and make Me the ultimate goal of life.'

(Lord Krishna in the Bhagavad-Gita, 6.11-14)

This is proper meditation. Breathing can be highly beneficial when followed the scriptural injunctions. The Bhagavad-Gita especially has been established since 5000 years and stood the test of time. Many humans have thus learned meditation, in a spiritual process.

The Breath is transforming material energy into spiritual energy, but what is the difference?

Spiritual energy is eternal, and material is temporary, therefore the matter of the life air being conscious means transforming dull matter into intelligent, living force.

This force always needs a proper fix-point to be directed and controlled. Therefore one shall always stare at the nose-tip. The nose tip or the space in-between lips and nose can be seen as the centre of mind, or even the pivotal point of all senses. When fixed, the life breath can control all the senses and sense organs.

Understanding the breath means work on ones own capacity to live fully. This life is meant for experiencing the higher states of consciousness, in bliss and happiness. This bliss and happiness comes as a natural and personal energy from within this heart. Every heart is the seat of a personality with unique character and individual perception. By breathing consciously, one can attain full understanding of this personality.

Self-awareness and satisfaction dawn, an experiencing that can be imagined as the sunrise. The light is always present, and especially beautiful before sunrise. The light already illuminated the earth, however the sun planet is just slowly moving across the horizon. When the full sun globe is visible it is the light that spreads across the earth to nurture and uphold the beings living on it.

All living beings are dependent on this light. Likewise all emanates from the personality. Ones character can fully shine when the personality is rising above the horizon of consciousness.

The eternal heaven of Dharma or 'Order' is the moral of life we experience. This eternal life is responsible for everything. It streams from a source very far and yet so close. This order brings also duality into play. Like the interplay of day and night, rise and fall, flood and ebb, likewise the breath has a dual character. Inhale and exhale.

Interestingly, this interplay is like a dance of lover and beloved. Inhale and exhale behave like two lovers in a dance, constantly inviting each other and separating. The matter of breathing in symbolizes the invitation of the lover to dance. When the inhale takes place, there is union, and for a moment, everything is within harmony. A small moment of unity resolves and the exhale ignites the separation, one lets go of the matter of breath and the dancing lovers symbolically part. A small moment passes within this separation and the whole dance begins again.

You are welcome to imagine the character and personalities behind the process as it is a valuable experience for everyone. Just be aware of the matter of life air, breath or sky and notice that all living beings are connected through this element. Likewise, all beings are sharing a similar technique or instrumentality of the breath. The simplicity behind it is most stunning, some even assume the whole macro-cosmic manifestation within the micro-cosmos of the breath.

Creation stories of ancient Scriptures confirm the subtle breath moving creation and making manifestation possible.

So let's create! A life full of bliss and harmony awaits. Breathwork includes a higher goal, which helps everyone at the same time a higher purpose brings a point of balance. It is said that the ultimate balance is a personality with form and character. This personality of supreme balance is full in all aspects, like eternity, wisdom and bliss.

When we focus our attention on the lotus feet of this personality, then one can experience a heartfelt protection light. Like a mother fosters her youngest child with care and attention.

This care and attention can be explored by everyone and further, one can experience unity.

Breathwork has been described since ancient yoga, around ten thousand years ago on earth, but this science is of eternal value and has no limit in its capacity, because it works with eternal principles of unity.

On this journey we embark on an exploration of the Self and the Highest values of life. By these ideals within the meditation the practitioner can slowly an safely overcome any difficulty. Specifically, modern diseases like depression, anxiety, fear and angst are arising due to forgetfulness of ones true and original position under the lotus feet of the Supreme Truth.

By implementing constant, conscious practice of meditation and yoga the practitioner can find shelter within the heart of bliss and consciousness. Here everything is bright and beautiful, within meditation. Meditation comes from the Latin word medius and refers to the middle. The centre of all spiritual energies are within the middle of the core of energy, commonly known as the soul. Here, one can experience an exceptional and blissful realm of goodness and connectivity.

The breath is leading us into this realm, breath by breath. By the mercy of present masters and tour guides that have explored this conscious link of consciousness, breath and eternal living spark, one can cross the oceans of material suffering and obtain the mercy of the Supreme.

This force is present within everyone, and everyone can learn to attain it. Even children, once receptive, can achieve great results through faithful practice.
This practice starts with listening, as you do, dear listeners and readers. The proper way is to listen attentively with an awake mind, that is seated within the senses. Once the ears are open and the mind still, the heart of unity can experience unity. From here it is present, and can be maintained. Breathwork also refers to the constant mode of balance where every state of emotional or intellectual endeavour finds a common ground of peace and harmony. This steadiness within pleasant and unpleasant circumstances arises due to faithful effort and steady practice by listening and applying.

The body in these terms acts as a vessel, and our mind and intelligence as a steering wheel and compass. The senses are like rudders that dig into the ocean of life. The air in that respect acts as a driving force to cross the waters by catching a good breeze. One who knows how to sail properly within this bodily vessel is able to cross beyond the condition of misery, suffering and pain to discover the lands of peaceful unity and bliss.

Breathwork is a journey. The vessel of our body must be steady and sturdy on this way, always align with the thoughts, words and actions we take. By breathing consciously one is in charge of all the functions that are connected to the energy current of life air, prana or breath.

This bodily vessel then can be put into a certain state of balance where matters like old age and disease aren't it effecting it anymore. There are many stories of breath-workers, Yogis and meditators that overcame old age and disease, habits of eating, sleeping and mating just through the constant meditation on the Supreme. These fixed-up meditators are said to become liberated, enlightened or just very old. This state of balance of the bodily vessel can be achieved by everyone through spiritual and meditative practice, like breath work.

True spiritual practice realizes: I am not the body, this temporary vessel. It recognizes the difference between eternal living soul living within the body, and the body shell which is just a vessel for this temporary life. This material condition also applies for the mind, memory and imagination. It is all good to be using the mind in effective ways, but when the mind uses you, it becomes a dictator and not a true spiritual expert boatman.

This expert is supposed to guide us beyond birth and death to the spiritual realm that is found within the heart. Here within the heart all desires and identifications sit. Also, the spiritual identity, which is eternal, full of wisdom and bliss. This is the true nature of every single living being. Endless bliss, wisdom and eternity.

Therefore, let us step on board to accompany the expert sailor on this journey across the temporary oceans of misery to gain new horizons of a spiritual world full of bliss and happiness.

We start by sitting properly and adjusting the spine. The breath is equal and audible, noticeably entering the nose tip and feelingly streaming into the nose and to the heart. Let the breath be constant and equal. Let the inhale equal the exhale and be aware of any slight difference. Listen and observe the breathing, streaming in and out again.

Now, with every breath, one can add a thought. This helps to focus the attention and momentum.

Breathe in; I am not the body. Let it sink in. Breathe out; I am not the mind. Stillness. Breathe in; I am eternity, breathe out; I am bliss. Be aware of the subtle stream of air and let it sink into the heart and soul.

The soul knows, and can easily identify with this. Now, start all over again, but continue for some while. Breathe in; I am not this body, breathe out; I am not this mind.

Breathe in; I am eternity, breathe out; I am bliss. (Repeat for two minutes)

Breathe naturally and notice the breathing.

Now slightly whisper the words. Breathe in; I am not this body, breathe out; I am not this mind.
Breathe in; I am eternity, breathe out; I am bliss. While the inhalation takes place, naturally let the gaze shift between the eyebrows and naturally continue with the silence.
Breathe in; I am not this body, breathe out; I am not the mind. Follow along. Breathe in; I am eternity, breathe out; I am bliss. Feel it, embrace it, and make it a state of consciousness. This is the most subtle layer of life, like the sky is very fine, it pervades everything, so does consciousness. The identification is like a cloud. These move across the horizon and cover the beautiful light of the sun, but no worries, they move and soon move along. An identification is just a temporary state of consciousness, however, there are states of consciousness that are eternal and blissful. These awake states are the ones that lead our life to highest human potential.

Relax, and listen to the voice guiding the meditation and making this clear. Pure like the sky these meditations shall uplift and nurture everyone likewise. Like the sky has a personality, also the Supreme goal of all meditations has a character. Ever eternal, full of wisdom and bliss. Pure like the sunshine, this personality helps us, if we wish. As we so desire, we can ask for spiritual truth and happiness, therefore this prayer serves as invocation to invoke auspiciousness and good success of all meditations.

'O Supreme Reservoir of all pleasure, balance and happiness, please grant this neophyte meditator to be successful and great in effort. May thy light shine our ways to the lands of eternity, wisdom and bliss. Please, let us cross the dark oceans of nescience to focus our full attention on the good in life. May all living beings be happy!'

To give the meditation and Breathwork a proper frame, one can repeat this invocation every meditation sitting, or Breathwork session. It helps to clear the intention and to focus on success of practice. To end any meditation session it is recommended to fold the hands together, in front of the chest, palms meeting and thumbs touching the heart space, breathing consciously in and out again. Sigh, close the eyes for a moment of stillness and give thanks and appreciation for all and for one. Oneself can now bow or ground by touching the earth with the forehead, one can also dissolve the session with music. Chanting a mantra like the Light Mantra help to solve the sessions.

Follow along:

I am the Light of the World,
I am the Light of the World,
I am, I am, I am the light of the world.

You are the light of the world,
You are the Light of the World,
You are, you are, you are the Light of the World.

We are the Light of the World,
We are the Light of the World,
We are, we are, we are the Light of the World.

Chant and repeat.
Rest and relax.

Meditations for Anxiety

The shores of a never ending Discovery offer fresh air to breathe and more. The discovery brings the explorers closer to themselves. Let's breathe through with the seafarers and hope for good winds. As the wind allows one to be able to move, one sets sail with the help of the life air, we breathe - we live.

Breathe and come along a journey where we explore the beauty of the breath. Can you hear it? It is with us. Inhale, Exhale. Can you hear the wind coming in and going out again? Can you feel the intensity of the air? The fresh, cool air, it allows us to live and explore. We can be in harmony with all. All is breathing and alive. Let's embrace that and follow the flow.

The water is the great connection.
I am water, you are water, we are all connected with the water. The water is us. One is with the soothing balance, the harmony and unity, as we are all on the same sea. Let's see and find how the water giant is doing.

Water is the element of emotions and by stilling the breath, one can still the emotional sea.

All craving and desire,
The will to aspire,
Crystal clear sapphire,
Beautiful like water and fire.
Let's hear the rhythm of the sea, See, one can feel the harmony.
Let the whales show you how to be, In Peace, Love and Unity.

One may see, in the depth of the ocean, there is pure serenity, no stress, no tension, just watery peace, a gentle reminder of who we are at ease - Peace.

The depth and darkness are one of a kind, yet this underwater kingdom shines with light. It is close to the shore in the Meditational sea, where bliss is essence and happiness to be.

We can dive into this sea and see it ourselves, the tranquility and peace are one of a kind. So prepare yourself with a breath and relax, because the more we relax, the deeper we dive.

In the air, under the Earth, in the Forest, and the sea,
Water is within and with us, to be.
We are waters as everyone is water, likewise connected with the elemental flow, springing from a source, growing up in water, rising to be born and living a life. The waters are ceaseless and always in flux, eternally adaptive and making us alive.

We can speak to the water and it listens to us, it is brave and tender at the same time. Water, is alive and always in flow, may give to understand, waters also know.
Knowing the form and shapes of life, we can see that water is always here for balance and harmony.
In the Vessel all are in Balance and harmony, within, waters make a way, we can be thankful for it each and every day.

Let's praise the water and give thanks for its delight, also when there comes fright. Water adjusts and reflects what is there, light of the moon shimmers and the water is in care.

This is life, and life is water. Water is life and thankful we can be. Appreciate every drop and in abundance it may show, water springs, and comes in a flow. The waters are here to heal and nurture our growth, may one be fostered and held with life.

Thank you water, for making us feel alive, even in the good, good night.
We arrive at the island of ease to see the peace and we are equally happy to see. We are smiling in gratitude and hopefully we have a glimpse. Though we can see, a question arises in ourselves.

What is even anxiety?

Be aware of the breathing, while you are relaxing the head, this may give steadiness and grace to your being. Relax the body and breathe. The breathing is equally coming in and going out again. It is in one harmonious flow.
The in- breath is our dear friend and the out-breath is our dear friend leaving us for a moment. Let's embrace this friend. Hello, welcome dear Breath, and Goodbye, dear Breath it is nice meeting you.
The breath is always with us, saying hello for the space we are in and entering into the nostrils, streaming into the body. Within the body our friend enters our bodily vessel.
It makes connection with our lungs, heart and other friends. The incoming breath is very well invited to also meet the belly. The belly is our common friend. Everyone knows the belly, as the friends meet together at the belly button, all the friends equally find themselves traveling back and forth, so the in-coming friend, the breath, now is saying hello to everyone, meeting and greeting the other friends, like the heart, the lungs, the belly, but also the cells and mitochondrion, as the breath can travel everywhere we can also meet the toes with the breath.

So the friends, the tippy toe and the breath meet, greet and have a connection. This connection is very fragile and soft, so come, it can be even just spontaneous. When these meetings are done, the wonderful friendship parts and the beautiful journey goes on. So the breath says goodbye, I will see you, and then travels back from the lungs, over the nostrils into the space again: where we call this exhale.

In the Space the breath is free to be.
From here, we are noticing the friendship and we are aware of the breath and with every single breath one can relax, or energize. However one likes.

What is the best medicine for anxiety?
Trust and good friends.

Relax your body and find yourself safe and secure in the space of love. Around you, you're being surrounded with a shimmer of light that glows and brings about peace and harmony. This light we breathe and we can feel.

The light of friendship is like the smile. You can see it as soon as you smile honestly, one smiles back. This light of your love, smiling, is the power of friendship. Let's embrace that and find ourselves calm, breathing, feeling and breathing fully out again. The breathing is equal and the in-breath matches the out-breath. The breathing is natural and the constant flow is audible. You can hear the breathing coming in and going out.

Now you can close your eyes and find yourself in this space of imagination where you sit comfortable on green moss so mild like a cushion and so soft that you sink into this place and it may be a place of peace and harmony. So as you are. Breathing in and equally breathing out again. There's nothing to worry about, we are just trusting the love of nature and the friendship of our breath as our breath is our long life friend.
Smile and say hello to the breath. Embrace the breath. And let the breath go again. It's a constant coming and going. And whatever is happening around you, find yourself always in balance with the breath as the rhythm goes.

The rhythm might be fast and one can notice if the life is fast right now in this moment, or the breath might be slow, maybe life might be of a slow moment right now.

So whatever moment is happening is happening in the breath. The breath is our friend and one might know when to say hello as the friend is coming again and again. And one also knows to welcome the breath with joy and with a smile.
Oh hello you wonderful breath of life, you are my friend coming home. Then there is space for celebration, for love and for life.

This is the life happening within you. When the life has happened we have to say goodbye again. This goodbye is a chance to make space and to let go, maybe this friend likes to go with the present.

Like here, bring the peace and take this love, and maybe here you have a smile for your way out. So we let go and the ever-lasting friends go away with love and peace and a smile. When your friend has left, there is enough space to embrace for another time your friend will come.

Breathe in and let your friend the life air come into the nostrils and let your friends go again leaving the nostrils. Every time we breathe we have the chance to equip our friend with a message, and whatever this message may be, one can come up with the one, message going into the world.

This is why we can speak in prayer for the world. This is why we can hope for friendship in the world. Hence we speak it out, in devotion and love. Let's pray.
May all beings be happy,
may all beings be at peace, may all beings be friends,
like the best friends one can be.
To enhance the potency of this prayer we can speak it louder and we can speak it more often, so one can repeat that prayer again and again.

May all beings be happy
May all beings be at peace
May all beings be friends.

So we are still sitting on the most in a beautiful friendship garden and in this garden there is much friendliness, even the birds, the bees and the trees. And so we could just sit here when all of the beings come to us, and we can greet them with a smile.

The beings smile back in this world's unity, in this garden the friendship is present. Let's also think about our real life friends, let's imagine them and invite them kindly with a smile. All we see, them smiling back and there we go, let's be together in this Garden of friendship.

The sun is shining and the weather is nice, we are able to enjoy the sound of the birds and the song of nature. It is like a concert just for us, the music is so beautiful and harmonious we find our balance here.

See now and it's a blessing, we are here. Now, let's embrace that and feel the breath again. Notice the breath streaming in the nostrils and out again, and find the rhythm to be equal, and the heartbeat in synchronicity.

This synchronicity brings balance and relief, it is like a shelter, coming home, to the garden of friendship. We can walk around now and search for something that is interesting for us. Maybe we find the tree with special leaves, or maybe we find a flower with this specific cense, but we do really, is just observing.

We see ourselves playing, we see ourselves wondering in the forest full of adventure, we are witnessing the constant stream of life, like rivers and water flow and our friends they like to be with us.
So together we are exploring this friendship garden, so together we are exploring our friendship, so together we are living in harmony. There is no fight, there's just the pulse of life, that makes us live and feel encouraged, and it makes us smile and happy to be who we want to be.

Let's embrace that and let's embrace the breath, let's embrace our friends and the place we are playing in.
This place is in our heart so let's embrace the heart. From this place, it also is in our minds so let's embrace the mind and the imagination. Let's embrace our friends and family and let's embrace the whole world as friends and family.

Now see yourself in this friendship garden and from your heart there is a silver light shining into the hands and the hands embrace each other, bringing the palms together, and now the light shines from the middle of your head into the wide wide world.

The balance spreads around the whole body and we become lighter and lighter.

We are becoming so light, we start to sink into our wonderful world of imagination where we can sit in a garden of friendship. This Garden of Friendship is free for us to be. We can invite all our friends or we can just sit in serenity. There is a nice cushioned grass patch for us, it is very soft and really inviting us for a meditation.

So we are sitting here, meditating with our bottom on the ground and we feel the soft grass on this lush field, there is also a tree, and we see, the tree greets us, too. Hello tree and beautifully the tree gives us shelter and a steady help to maintain peaceful and calm, this is what trees do, staying peaceful and calm. Beautiful isn't it? The tree is obliged and greets us with a smile, we smile back.

We are all breathing the same air, and look up into the air, there was just a fresh rain shower and now the sun comes along again, what a wonderful surprise the moisture in the air and over the field creates a haze where the sun shines through and there we have a glimpse of a multicoloured rainbow, shining and bowing to us, oh Hello, dear friend, I am the Rainbow; Welcome!

The rainbow bows at our feet and we are just seeing a lovely rainbow, that invites us with many beautiful colours, tender red, and golden orange, shiny yellow, bright green, light blue, indigo, and violet.

All the colours are now with us, greeting us one by one, always bowing and Saying, Hello I am indigo, Hello, I am golden Orange, Hello, I am bright Green; and everyone smiles and we smile back.
The rainbow welcomes us for a walk and we can walk with the rainbow to see, where does this rainbow come from, yes, we Can show you. I am coming from the source. I am a rainbow born from the light, and born from the wonderful world.
May all beings be friends, playing in the friendship garden. May all beings be happy, may all be at peace.

So let's find the breath again and the breathing goes in and out, with saying hello to the breath and with a goodbye we are letting the breathing go. Everything is in harmony and now in this friendship garden we have time to celebrate, so let's bring everyone together and celebrate this friendship.
The birds are bringing their favourite songs, the elephants are bringing their favourite trumpets, the monkeys are bringing their favourite drums, the ducks are bringing their favorite dress. The trees that bring their favourite flowers and the flowers bring their favourite cense. The bees are bringing their favourite honey and all the friends are coming together.

There is a wonderful celebration for the sunset, waiting for the night as the sun brought his favourite friends the moon. And the moon brought her favourite friends the stars, and the stars brought their favourite friends the Stardust. In this Stardust is a wonderful dream to the nice night as it is coming just while the sun sets.

All the animals, all the people, all the flowers and the insects as well as the sun and the moon are now watching and we are here to all speak a prayer together:

May all beings be happy
May all beings be free of anxiety
May all live in harmony in this friendship garden.

We are gently closing the night as everyone gently says goodbye with a smile, we also smile and put our palms together again to give thanks. We close our eyes and are content with this wonderful friendship garden where we can return every time even in the night.
Now relax your whole body and feel the life of your breath slowly and gently calming and becoming smooth. Now find yourself in peace and harmony with all the beings around.

May it be a good night. May the stars shine bright, it's the moon singing a song for peace and harmony. Rest relax and sleep well.
Everything in life is free,
the friendship, the breathing, the peace and harmony.
We come to this life
With the help of the light. From the stars and sun,
Life can sprout and begun.
Everything in life is free, The stars and the sun, The peace and harmony, To hold it dear kind,
Is just a state of mind, To bring it forth and go, We are the one to know.

Everything in life is free,
The peace, love and harmony.

Let's remember once more the beautiful discovery in this garden of friendship and how all the beings can be friends, peaceful and calm like the tree, in colourful serenity, the tender red, golden orange; shiny yellow, bright green, light blue; indigo and violet: all are here for friendship and for life, like the breath, making one feel alive. All the parts of the body are now in connection, in peace and serenity. There is now wholesome balance and harmony, from the tippy toes to the head, as are full in rest.

May All the beings be happy and free, in the colourful world of harmony, May my friendship be with all, all the beings may be friends,
May the love and peace surround the whole world for good life.

May there always be light, even in the darkest night,
May our happiness and joy shine bright even in the darkest night, May we greet the moon and the stars with a smile,
May ones happiness last for a while:
May all the beings be safe and sound, in peace, in love and harmony. May I come back to the breath and to the body,

To fully engage in the life right here, right now. Chant and be happy.
I am the light of the world:
I am the light of the world;

I am, I am; I am the light of the world.
You are the light of this world,
You are the light of this world;
you are; you are; you are the light of this world.
We are the light of this world, we are the light of this world, we are we are, we are the light of this world.
May all be friends; may all be the light, even in the darkest night.

Reiki Self-Treatment

Stored emotions in our root chakra affect our well-being, for higher possibilities of joyfulness and peace.
Ask the universal life force, Reiki, to withdraw energy. Ask Reiki for Guidance. Be aware of the principles, and sit comfortably within a space of love and security. Find the right hand hovering on your feet as you are sitting cross-legged, or in your lap when laying down put your right hand on the right thigh. The left hand comes to the heart space. Imagine a beautiful stream of flowing energy from one hand to the other up, and down, and in- between the two hands, for the betterment of any stored emotions, hold the position for a few minutes and bring both hands to the heart space, putting your hands safely on the chest. Feel and breathe, feel the breath.
The heart center is the point of spiritual balance. Naturally, balance comes when you are out of stress when there is no rush and no struggle.
This can happen when you focus your attention, either to your heart center, to the breathing, and to your hands. The heart chakra promotes harmony and well-being, so intentionally hold this position for a few minutes and make sure to breathe equally.
In and out.

Meditation for Deep Sleep:

Prepare yourself for a deep relaxation of body mind and spirit. This meditation will include a full body relaxation where we start from the head bringing awareness to the bottom of the feet, scanning and relaxing the whole body. While relaxing the whole body, the mind might wander Yet one might focus on the breath and the part where the breathing goes into the nostrils, to maintain awareness. When the mind wanders we can always come back to the breath.

Gently and naturally be aware of the breath coming in and going out. You are a life and you can be thankful to be a life. While preparing just bring your body in a relaxed posture preferably laying down on your back having your legs shoulder width apart and the hands on the side of the body palms facing up. One might be covered with a blanket and cushioned with a pillow on the necessary parts.

This is a deep relaxation, so you might be able to lose your focus and to be in total tranquillity for the whole time of this meditation.

Let's start by relaxing the whole body, from the head, you feel the top of the head, just relax the head. You feel the forehead and the muscles around the eyes, now let go of the pressure around the eyes, around the jaw, along the mouth, just letting go of all the pressure relaxing with every single breath.
Just relax your throat, breathe, and just relax your shoulders.
Imagine all the weight from your shoulders lightens with every breath.
The way of the breath lightens the whole being and you come to the arms bringing awareness to them. Be aware of the arms and the arms are relaxing. The elbows and wrists are equally relaxing with every breath. You are noticing the hands and the palms of the hands, and with the awareness the hands relax.

 With the awareness, constantly breathing, the chest will relax. Just keep the breathing and stay equanimous, with the breathing the inner organs will relax. Feel the breath coming in into the lungs, around the heart and all around the body. Now be aware of the belly, breathing and feeling the belly relaxes with every breath. One is sinking into the ground becoming heavier and heavier and letting go of all the stress and pressure. All the tension dissolves into air or finds its grounding into the floor.

 It is all energy. With the relaxation the energy can flow and harmonize with the ground and with the energy around you. In the air and in the earth there's balance. This balance is spreading all around the belly, around the chest and around the head. With every breath the relaxation is sinking deeper and deeper into Ones being. Even all the muscles around the hips and at the bottom of your spine, are now with awareness and relaxing.

Ones attention is the root of energy, now at the spine. This is where peace and harmony as well as deep relaxation stem. Here, we can imagine a beautiful, lush red flower blooming and showing the blossom of wonderful red petals spreading into every direction, equally the relaxation is spreading evenly in the whole body.

One relaxes legs and knees, the lower thighs and ankles as well as the feet, are now filled with awareness. We breathe into this and with the awareness and the breath you are bringing relaxation. This relaxation spreads even into the tippy toes. Here we let the energy rise again and we just notice and be aware of all the body parts.

Whatever sensation arises we stay evenly in balance. Notice the legs, fully notice the legs and relax. Notice the hips at the bottom of the spine, fully notice the hips at the bottom of the spine, and relax. Notice the lower back and fully notice every vertebrae of the spine and relax. Notice the upper back and fully notice the neck and the back of the head. Relax and sink deeper and deeper with every single breath, the body becomes lighter and lighter. The whole body is now light and one can feel the blossom of the flower, so light the whole body is equally relaxed from the head to the toes, the relaxation spreads from the belly into every cell of the body.

The whole body is rooted in relaxation and bliss. A beautiful light grounds one from bottom of the spine and the red flower turns into a beautiful flower of light protecting one from head to toe. Sheltering one for a good, deep relaxation. Equally breathe and feel the breath relaxing one from the head to the toe, all surrounded by a protective light. Whenever one feels ready, the breath can take us deeper or it can release the relaxation,
just notice again the body parts and see how every body part is awakening with the energy of the breathing, coming and going, we focus on the entrance of the nose again and help ourselves to a nice massage or soothing music.

Body Scan

Come to full relaxation by giving yourself space. The whole body is on the ground. The whole body relaxes. Breathe through, sigh of relief and feel the firm ground. Nothing you need to do, nowhere you need to go, just relax and feel the sensations of your body. Be aware that this is Yoga Nidra, the conscious sleep. Stay aware by listening deeply to the voice. As we go through the different parts of the body with our awareness, we stay awake. The body relaxes fully and we close our eyes. Remain aware of the natural flow of respiration. The natural flow coming in and out. Coming in and flowing out. Feel the sensations, whatever it may be, vibrating, tingling, itching, warmth or cold, lightness or numbness, whatever it may be, you remain aware of the natural breath, entering on the nose tip. Let the breath flow and whenever you lose yourself in thoughts, come back to the breath entering in and out. We start scanning and wandering with our awareness from head to feet. By doing so we relax.
Start to be aware of the top of your head, feel the top of the head, relax the top of the head, the top of the head is relaxed. Let the awareness sink slowly into the skull area, the back of the head and into the face. Be aware, feel and relax. Be aware of the forehead, the nostrils, the jaw, the mouth and chin. Feel every little part and let go. Relax. Be aware of the shoulders and neck area, around the throat. Feel the whole shoulder girdle, the neck area and throat. Be aware and feel, any sensation we just observe, just observe, feel and relax. Head area we relax, relax the whole head area of the body. Let the awareness sink into the chest area, around the heart, feel and be aware of the tiny muscles evenly pumping blood into the heart, be aware of the rhythm of your breathing and your heart beat. Observe and feel any sensation coming up. Give space and relax all the chest area, all the chest is relaxed.

Balance Meditation

Find a comfortable seat, bringing your whole body into balance between earth and sky. You can sit or lay on the ground in a comfortable place. Watch your breath coming equally in and out. Working with the breath is the one fundamental trust, as we live, we breathe.

Come to terms with your body, come to ease, settle, there is nothing to fear, relax, with a voice that is guiding you into meditation.
Just trust the breathing as it is coming and going, gently notice the breath and be aware of the sensation of the breath entering the nostrils and leaving them again.

Equally in and out again, breathe and be aware how it comes into your nose tip, into your body and into your heart.

Here in the heart the breath is home. The beloved invites the lover and everything comes home. One can notice there is awareness in the breath which is bringing us home into the body and into the heart.

We notice every part of the body, from the heart to the belly, to the spine, to the shoulders and head, and even to the tippy toes. Feel how the heart is opening and chest is widening. Here in the heart is where the eternal spark of light resides.

Breathe out all you are letting go and receive all you breathe in. One can make up a thought, we are letting go, and we can make up a thought that we receive, therefore we can inhale I Am Trust, and exhale all that we are not. Breathe, in I am Trust and breathe out again. Continue on and know that the thought and words travel with the breath, into your heart.

Find peace and relax the body, coming to a state of trust and harmony.

With every single breath one is becoming lighter and lighter. I am Light travels with the breath and comes into every cell of the body. The whole body is now very light and even so light it starts to float and lifting of the ground, just with the help of the breath.

The body is so light and trusting the body floats into the space of Trust, the whole body is now fully in a space of trust and peace. Feel the ease, the small breeze from the air entering the nose and coming to the heart.

In our imagination we can see a nice tender space where we can land again for good care, like in a flower field, full of moss and soft ground, landing there it feels like we are home in a space of trust and balance.

Feel the balance of the breath, equally inhaling and exhaling, as the thoughts arise we can just notice them like we notice the leaves dancing in the wind.

See the beautiful wind playing with the trees, also these trees are giving us shelter and equanimity, just trust and find a nice space close to that tree.

The trees are holding up the earth and likewise we can hold trust within us, just steady and always growing up towards the sky.

Embrace nature and feel the rhythm of the breath, find the heart and maybe there is a friend who likes to join us.

Do you have a friend you like to see? Invite this friend with a smile into your light space of heart.

To trust means to have full faith in goodness in person.

Whatever will be, everything turns out just for a reason. Therefore always be thankful and happy for all the little things. Even watch the flowers who are so happily growing on the field providing nectar for the bees, and see the trees?

Do they ever complain? Still and steady they hold on for days and days on end, especially when there is a good friend. Walking along the small stream, the water is crystal clear and there is a fish or two within the river that flows into a lake.
 Finding a reflection in the lake, one can see a mirror face of the wonderful surface, within this endless space.

Holding the moment of trust, even when there is no doubt, no lack and desire to be somewhere else, that is balance and trust.

Giving a hand to someone, and see there is a smile that illuminates the world, that is trust. Even together or just being alone, that is trust. Know to be content even when there is a surprising event, like a dancing tree.

Without any fault everything finds a place on this earthly surface, even the rain. All come the same, yet we trust and have everything we need. A shelter is right there. All in care, just trust and see, everything is in divine harmony.

Life is miraculous and wonderful as sometimes unexplainably we just trust and see the magic unfold within the matter of the now, breathing and opening our hearts for the grace of goodness, one shall receive the mercy of the light.

In Peace, Love and Unity, knowing everything is in divine harmony. Breathe equally.

Notice the subtle sensation of the thoughts and the breath coming to terms with the light, knowing everything shall be alright. The perfect harmony is here, within the heart of everyone.

The flowers and the trees, the friends and families all together like to live in harmonies. All are the same in their goal to come back home.

Where the heart is there is bliss, and all longing to never miss a chance of meeting someone new, just trust and what we will do? Smile and breathe, greet as a friend always and forever one to be.

Then, all shall be happy.

Within the whole body there is now the light of trust spreading and we can know that all living entities are seeking the same light of trust, and trust is everywhere and there and within the heart. Like there is air within the space there is love for all in the face of a smiling heart.

We are all a part of this world. Even when the sun sets for a goodbye it shall still shine, let's embrace the stillness of the lake one more time and see the setting suns face shining for a good night over the hills and within the heart, all we are a part.

This space is here and now for us to feel, from the tippy-toes to the head, to the chest and all around the nose, with the jaw and around the neck, the arms, shoulders and hands are relaxed, as well as the finger tips and the lips, the jaw and the neck.

The whole body is filled with lightness and trust, as we breathe there is no must, but we can do, whatever there is to do! We can also trust! Where there is no must, just let be, and feel free to also renounce and come back home to the premises of the body where the soul finds its heart.

There, everything is a start and we begin to breathe.
Be aware of the breath and let it flow naturally, just be aware of the body and relax from the head to the toes. The sunshine is now all gone, yet one can see the reflection within the sky, that is coming in beautiful colours and o 'wonder why we deserve to be blessed. Of course, because we trust.

Let's adjust the body to find a comfortable way, of trusting our close ones each and everyday, maybe invite them for a dream with the heart-full space of trust, giving oneself to the best.

Give thanks and appreciation to the best ones close by, and be grateful for every single breath, as it comes naturally, we give thanks to nature accordingly.
All the appreciation to the world family.

May all beings be happy and live in equanimity.

Now, close the eyes and see yourself, just sitting in a nice tranquil state of equilibrium. This beautiful light of love surrounds you, and here you can take shelter, with all the joy and gratitude.

Maybe now, you can see yourself from head to toe, from toe to head, and again from head to toe. Nice light surrounds you and helps you to grow.

As the sun shines we all need light to grow, for a moment we can see our friends and family within this world. With light and growth. Smile and greet all the known faces.

Be aware again of the heart and be aware of the breath. This is your shelter, and only you know the truth within your heart, so does every person know the truth within their hearts.

Let the truth shine, and just relax, as a smooth chant can help purify and prepare for the night.

I am the Light of the World,
I am the Light of the World,
I am, I am, I am the Light of the World.

You are the Light of the World,
You are the Light of the World,
You are, you are, you are the Light of the World.

We are the Light of the World,
We are the Light of the World,
We are, we are, we are the Light of the World.

Be happy and smile

Rest, relax and find shelter within eternity. Trust is with you.

So find a comfortable position and imagine your spine. You see the spine, vertebrae for vertebrae and there is also a root, imagine, the root coming from the lowest bottom of the spine and spreading throughout the soil, into the layers of the ground. That ground then is the fundament for our balance.
So we breathe, and breathe in the balance. Equally in and out, Balanced breath, equally in and out.

All in harmony and balance, the breathing flows naturally and the body is align with all the elements. As the spine is straight, we are relaxing our jaw and head. We can let go of any tension, to relax and ease, into a smile.

Breathe and smile, gently.
Breathe and be in balance.
Like the roots of a tree, we find steadiness in the ground.
And we can also tone a sound, that helps us to relax.

Lets open our mouth, wide and full, on AHHH, hold the sound as long as possible. AHHHH
Now breathe again and find the balance and harmony, in the ground, and of course we can tone another sound.

This time for our heart, the Sound goes UHHHH, very mild and long, we can tone this once more, UUHHHH and there you connect to your heart and now lets embrace the smile, lets connect to our head with HUMMMM, long and gently, sound HUMMMMM. These three sounds, AHHH, UHHH, HUMMM are the essential building blocks of life.

Like a tree has a seed, that's the AAH, it also has a stem, that's the UHH, and of course it has a crown and that's the HUMMM. All together these three sounds AUM give the primal sound, a wonderful invention.

The trees are mostly silent, but they can understand all the sounds of the universe, therefore we always have to be conscious what we say in our environment, as we are peaceful, breathing and meditating, the environment, the trees and all the other beings are very happy with us.

Of course we can smile and find our happiness within our heart. There, a wonderful lotus flower blossoms and we see, that everyone's lotus flower is the same, yet different.

Everyone is breathing the same air, yet we are all different from the inside.

All the trees are of the same structure, yet, every tree is one of a kind. Isn't that beautiful?

Let's relax and find out how the trees are embracing the night.

A tree doesn't really need to close the eyes to sleep, yet knows exactly when the sun is setting, therefore around this time, the tree gives everything into the atmosphere, to celebrate and cheer the great gift of life.

Sometimes, a lot of flowers are coming from a tree, sometimes, the tree dances in the wind to find expression, and sometimes the fruits of a tree are growing from just a little seed.

One seed has all the information a tree needs to live on for thousands of years, and even in the nights, the trees are growing upwards and downwards, isn't that interesting?

As all the beings, like the trees are part of this world, we are also growing in the night, yet, we have to be sure, that we are relaxed and ready for the upcoming night. Therefore the trees prepared a nice soothing song for the upcoming good night.

It is again, around that time, where everything sets, from the shine, of the sun, to the son, of a kingdom divine.

Please, enjoy the moment, and breathe, like we are here together to live.

Enjoy the moment and breathe, The air comes in and out, There is so much doubt,

But leave it all behind,

Be sure and one shall find,

That there is more to the dark,

That there is always a spark,

That ignites the wisdom of life.

Even in thought we respect the light,

We know, it must be night, Whenever we are in sight,

we arrange to be alright,

With a song, that goes all night long.

Sing it and feel it in the breath.

Sing it and feel it in the air,

Breathe and be enjoying the now. Everything is in care, just trust, just trust. There is no more, do's or must.

Just relax and keep the breath, Feel the peace and the ease.

Root yourself to the ground,
And hear the beautiful sound.
It is the air, in the space,
Now imagine a face,
Let it be kind and smile,
Hold it on for a while,
Enjoy the sight,
For a good, good night.

In the moment we listen to the trees, we are also listening to our selves, conscious and wise, we are all rooted on the same earth.

Be kind and bring your friends, to this wonderful kingdom of peace and harmony. Enjoy every bit of it.
Rest and sleep well.

We can breathe safety and protection. With every inhale there comes safety and with every exhale we let go the uncertainty. We inhale security, and let go uncertainty with the exhale. Breathe and feel the security coming to you, and the uncertainty leaving you, more and more we relax and find space to smile.

Let's be happy and celebrate life as it is. Even in this night there certainty, tomorrow the sun will rise, as always, we give thanks to our Mothers and Teachers that help us on our path and we thank Mother Earth for Life.

We now relax our body, with every breath, there comes upon relaxation, of the body, and mind. We are relaxing the head, the head is relaxed, breathe equally in and out, now relax the neck and throat, the neck and throat shall relax, we breathe in and out.
Now let's relax the shoulders and arms, elbows, palms and fingertips, breathing in and out, the shoulders, arms, elbows, palms and finger tips relax.

We shall relax the chest and upper body, inhaling and exhale, we do so. We shall relax the belly and lower back, inhaling and letting go with the exhalation. The whole of the upper body is now relaxed.

Now breathe and relax the thighs, legs, knees, ankles, feet and tippy toes, all the parts of lower body relax with the next inhale and exhale the whole body is relaxed.
Now we calm our thoughts, as we imagine a beautiful light giving us protection and security, this light fulfills our heart and blossoms like a wonderful lotus flower.

This Lotus flower shines in the most wonderful colours and protects us. The light reaches every parts of the body, every cell and we see ourselves in this light, engulfed and surrounded with a healing light of security.

Put your palms together and feel the harmony and security. Feel good and let the breathing be natural. Like a lotus flower, you can now open your hands and bring them to your lotus eyes. Surround your eyes with the healing energy of the hands and let your eyes bathe in the palms of your hands.

Breathe, equally in and out. Breathe, just naturally.
Maybe sigh, or massage your head, around the eyes and your jaw to feel totally fine. All is now safe and sound, with a smile we are ready for a good, good night.
Rest, and relax completely.

Let's find a comfortable position, where we are align with the ground and with the sky. Come to ease in that position and gently close your eyes. Let it be like a window opening for the holy altar.
There, on this altar you see many beautiful deities and pictures of saints, like great masters and mystical beings.

See yourself sitting in this holy place and find ease, watching the candle lights and smelling the incense, so fragrant and nice, the whole room is filled with joy and happiness. It is secure and safe, therefore we don't have to worry about anything. Just breathe, equally in and out, see the air flowing in regularly, and constant, and see it flowing out, regular and constant.

One is safe, to be breathing means to be in the security of life. Here in the body, we are safe, here in the sacred room we are safe, here with a guide and teacher we are safe. Feel the shelter and open your heart, like a lotus flower. Let this lotus flower bloom and see every petal of this lotus flower adjust to the light.

The light shines from your heart and illuminates the room, the petals of the lotus flower open and one is surrounded by this lotus flower light.

Did you know, that lotus flowers even grow in the deepest swamps, where there is hardly pure water and light? Yet, the lotus flower remains unspoiled and graceful in-midst this nature.

Let's go for a soothing and mild walk down the forest lane to find a swamp with many lotuses. There we see the trees opening up a way for Us, the alley leads straight to a little muddy swamp, where we find a wooden floor.

Let's wait here and see the flowers in the distance.

With shimmering silver and purple the petals of the lotuses surround the yellow golden middle, the stigma. It is a splendid wonder to look at, but how can the lotus flower feel safe in this swamp, so dark and moist?

In a subtle and clear voice the purple-golden Lotus says:
I am secure, when I am within me, as the sun light comes, I open up. I trust, the sunlight is my benefactor bringing me growth.

As the Lotus explains the ways to come to a place of security we share a human place of security we call home, this home is the place where we find community and joy in the things we do, together with our loved-ones, we live here, work, study and find shelter.

In a beautiful kingdom, that longed to be at peace,
We can explore and walk around the forest at ease. There also is a teacher and when we kindly ask, please.
Give us an answer to our questions, bring us release,
The teacher may illuminate the darkness into light.
As long as there is no fight, we are alright.
Let's enjoy this little bit of life, feel and shine bright.
Even, when we have to say goodbye the day and hello to the night.

In nature it is always good to spend

Life is beautiful as is it is - let's pray

So shall it be for every time and day Let's connect Ourselves to the good way.
Every drop of rain feels so fine and okay. I might be happy, and in harmony,
With the flowers, the rain, the soil and sun,
I feel like life is blooming and just has begun.
Every breath one takes there Is possibility to awake
Let's enjoy the travel and give the night a chance,
Prepare with simple breathing and just feel fine and ok.
Like you are laying in a bed of flowers, so soft and tender you sink in, and with every breath there is more space to relax, let's relax into the breath to sink more and more into the bed of flowers. The wonderful feeling holds on and one listens to the breathing, slow and rhythmic in harmony with the body and mind.

Keep the breathing equal and fine and try not to think to much, just enjoy the bed of flowers, Let yourself sink and feel how the body is becoming lighter and lighter, Like a butterfly we become smaller and smaller, we can sense the lightness of the body which transforms into a small, tiny speck of light. We are now this light and it is so light you can be as light as light itself.

Feel the ease and surround yourself with the comfort of the night. Slowly we sense the breathing again and nice fresh air flows into the body, and the light returns back to the bed of flowers.

One is there, just breathing and we invite one of our best friends to come along into the beautiful flower garden with us, there we can roam and play for a while until we are again coming back to our selves.

Just imagine the free space and endless lush field in your imagery flower garden, where a bed of flowers and a friend always wait for you, go and enjoy the space.
When there is the moment to come back, we reconnect with the body and breathe again. The breath is the bridge between the imagery world and the body.

Just breathe and now the breath is always with you, like a good friend, that comes along on a journey to travel with you. Patiently and persistently breathe and feel the ease.

With every breath the lightness within the body spreads from the heart, the centre of light, into the whole body. Breathing in and out, equally, will bring balance to the whole body and there we find the space to relax and imagine.
It is like the soil,
The breath,
Like the rain that comes,
The in and out,
It is the flower that grows, Oh, the Nature knows.
The rhythm equal and steady, Are you ready?
Say goodbye to the flower lady and follow along to have a nice soothing sleep on your flower bed.
All these have space to hold the earth in place and when human found a happy face, it was for all worlds pace.

A simple way to be is loving just like this simple sensation of the sun beams can make us smile and happy, even the simple sensation of the life's air can make us equally happy.

This feeling can evolve and grow into trust and love, like a small seed grows into the a nice and blossoming tree of harmony.

Let's embrace the situation and continue on for a relaxation that brings us closer to our eternal seed of love, which resides in our heart. We shall now nurture this seed with the acceptance and loving kindness that we hold for the whole world. May all beings equally be happy and at peace. Find ease.

The breathing is coming and going, just like the sun shine or waves at the ocean, it can also sound like the sea. Can you hear, the breathing comes and goes again, remain equal and notice the breathing carry us closer to the heart.

Here in the heart space, there is a garden full of compassion and kindness, with growing flowers of love and devotion, with equal means we approach the garden and find a nice spot for a new seed.

It shall be a very blessed seed, that allows us to accept and tolerate all the desires, thoughts, feelings and emotions that ever come, just like a mountain accepts the greatest winds and weather.

Be aware of the nice spot within your heart space garden, and chose wisely as it may be an eternal tree that lasts forever. This blessed seed can now be sown. We get our hands into the earth and make a little cave, there one sets the seed and gives it a sweet smile.

This seed shall grow, with all the benefits and blessings, for the whole wide world. May all beings be happy.

Now cover the seed and equally distribute the water of nourishment and compassion. It is coming from a copper cup and can equally be used for all the elements of nurturing the seed.

As we come to terms with love, it is giving love to anyone and everything, but principally to the roots of all things.
As we water the roots of any plant, to make it grow, one shall water the roots of love.
Compassion and kindness help us to be equally loving to anyone and everyone, because we are all part of the same soulful soil.

This equality is the balance within the water and now as we have sown and watered we shall give the light of understanding and wisdom to this everlasting plant of love.

Know love to be always there, within the heart, within the garden of your identity, love is always present, just like the soulful light of the sun, moon, and blessed beings.

Whenever there is a doubt, then one can just come back to the heart space where love and light reside, and surely one should always recite:

I am the Light of the World

Be aware again of the heart and be aware of the breath. This is your shelter, and only you know the truth within your heart, so does every person know the truth within their hearts.

Let the truth shine, and just relax, as a smooth chant can help purify and prepare for the night.

I am the Light of the World,
I am the Light of the World,
I am, I am, I am the Light of the World.

You are the Light of the World,
You are the Light of the World,
You are, you are, you are the Light of the World.

We are the Light of the World,
We are the Light of the World,
We are, we are, we are the Light of the World.

Evenly one can exchange Love with Light as it is equal.
I am the Love of this world,
You are the Love of this world,
We are the love of this world.

Embrace the sound and the voice, as they express love.

Just be happy and find love within the heart.
Chant and share your love.

Come to the heart space, rest and relax.

May all beings be happy.

<u>The source within the Heart</u>

Breathe and be aware of the heart space. Here, in the heart, all energies meet and create balance. Balance is key for Meditation.

One can have balance through an equanimous sitting position, and according to the matter of the breath.

Balance is like a mountain. Very firm and steady.
Just be a mountain, and whatever comes, thoughts, distractions, itching, trembling, pain, just be steady and keep the meditation very equally and peacefully.

Just inhale and be aware of the little pause between the in-and out-breath. Be aware of the subtle sensation of the breath moving into the nostrils and moving out again. Just simply be steady and aware, that the breath is connecting us to all the life. In consciousness, there is no difference between gold, stone, wood, water, and other things. They are all-natural matter. Even sensations like tickling, itching, vibrating, warmth, cold, are all the same, rising and passing.

Like a wind sweeps over the land and makes many trees dance, but the mountain remains steady. Be that mountain. A mountain is a steady magnet. Just attract goodness, by being a magnet for pure goodness. Uttering sacred syllables and affirmations help to get through the storm, yet one has to focus and face any difficulty. Easily, then one attracts beauty, wealth, fame, wisdom and so on.

Just breathe equally and hold the key balance. Sit on the feet of the Supreme Balance in Person and be aware of the heart. Here, within the heart wonders are happening. By breathing consciousness travels along the channels of energy from the outside to the inside. Within, in the heart, the air can unfold and circulate. Here, balance finds its expression. Notice the little pause even so after the exhale. Stillness takes care of the necessary space within the heart and the flowers of the garden of the heart can blossom to attract nectar-hunting honey bees.

Just be aware of the inhale, equal, and the exhale, equal. Find yourself in this wonderful space where the grass is very soft and lush, there are colourful cows grazing peacefully on the field and one can see the juicy green fields along the garden where nice desire trees are cultivated.
A gardener takes good care of all the plants by removing the weeds of ignorance. By conscious breathing one can, little by little, remove these weeds to get rid of fatigue, greed, pride, envy, and lust. This garden is a sacred space to meditate and there is even so the everlasting lake of consciousness just in near sight. A sunny morning provides wonderful and auspicious perspectives of the sunlight reflecting the whole spectrum of colours.

Notice the lake of consciousness and be aware of its state. Is it still? Is it fickle? How is this pure lake behaving? Slowly lean towards the lake and see your reflection within the waters. How are you seeing yourself?

Reflect and contemplate, lean back and relax within the meditative garden of your heart. Here, one can also plant the seed of good fortune. By addressing the divine feminine, the aspect of you that sets free fertility and purity.

Be aware of the subtle sound of the breathing and just remain like the steady mountain beyond the fields and meadows. The garden is waiting for a special seed, a desire-seed.

So, whatever you desire, you can cultivate. It takes time to plant, but at the right moment, one can implement a good seed in good soil.

Whatever you wish for, be clear about it, check it and nurture this wish like your little child. Be aware of this phenomenon that brings life to sprout. Whatever it may be, hold your hands together and think about a seed that likes to grow.

One can plant abundance, happiness and wealth, by giving all these to the Supreme Balance offering it with love.
' Please, let this desire-seed sprout into wealth, abundance and happiness.'
Then, one can put it into the ground of the hearts garden.

Just envision how a simple seed can grow into a full blossom tree, full of lively blossoms and an abundance of fruits. Just see the shapes, colours and luminescence emanating from that growing tree. However, it needs time to ripe, the desire can sprout very wonderfully.

Breathe and be equipoised just knowing that everything is already in place. Similar to a tree, one needs to find deep roots in meditation to attract fruitful results.

Protection Meditation

Just sit comfortably and witness the breathing coming in and out, be aware of the subtle sensations of the life air which is transferred to the heart. Here it is transformed into life force or prana, the subtle current of energy that makes the universe move.

By controlled breathing or pranayama, one can attract consciousness, through focus and determination one can deliberately open the gates of consciousness to set forth a river of energy. This source of this river and lake of emerging conscious energy or prana is the Supreme Origin, the source of all attraction.

See the Supreme Abundance sitting with very beautiful garlands and silks on the patio, along with many servants and playmates. Some musicians recite beautiful verses and there is one who is constantly fanning the Supreme Person who sits comfortably on a throne of finest gold and jewels.

Within the moment the Supreme Personality is fully satisfied and so shall we be. Be aware, and happy to be alive. It is a blessing and a gift to live and have control over one's actions. Be aware of little sensations. Sit very comfortably and notice the body, full of awareness and in balance. The breathing goes in and out, equally, inhale and exhale hold a little gap in-between. Just notice the length of the inhale, be aware of the gap, then exhale and notice the length of the exhalation. Start all over and balance in and exhale, so they are of equal strength and length.

Don't force, let every breath flow naturally and consciously. Let the spine be erect and the chest wide and in harmony with the upper and lower body. Proper sitting is the means of perfect meditation. Cross-legged in the lotus posture is the prime of all Meditation positions, but meditation can work everywhere and with everyone.

Just sit comfortably and notice the buttocks on the ground, feel the spine erecting and straightening up, until one reaches the head where skull, jaw and neck are in alignment. The shoulders are relaxed. The muscles around the eyes are soft, if not, and this happens in daily life, one can massage the skin and muscles around the eyes. Rotate the eyes clockwise and shift your gaze from left to right, up and down. Circle again. This serves as a calibration of the gaze which is highly important.

This gaze shall be straight with an equanimous mind. Leave the eyes half open and half closed, be aware of the gaze naturally shifting towards the inner eye, the space between the eyebrows. Naturally, one can perceive an inner vision of the Supreme Balance, the origin of all consciousness. Here, one might also see a lake that is still and pure, that is the lake of consciousness. From this lake, all energies flow into life, and whatever gate, or doorway we open, the energy flows into this channel. This is how attraction finds a path of expression. This is how conscious energy becomes manifest.

One has to know what gate or doorway to open.

For now, be guided and aware of the gates of protection opening. The gatekeeper, a servant of the Supreme Balance, unlocks the power of will and sets free a stream of energy into the channel of protection. Protection is a simple and effective energy that surrounds us since time immemorial. Humans have sought shelter and protection wherever in history, and now we can imagine a great forest grove of ancient sequoia trees, the giant mammoth trees of the World, spanning a life of over 2500 years.

Hereunder such a tree, one can find an imaginative shelter and protection. The tree is very humble and wise to give shelter and so it has been the mercy of the forest grove to shelter us for this moment.

Breathe equally in and out, and be aware of the subtle nature of the forest. Strong and mighty these trees give confidence and patience, protection and peace. Just reciprocate and receive the eternal service of nature here on earth. With great trunks and huge energetic branches, the balance is upheld and energy can flow easily in these channels.

Be conscious and know that the Supreme Origin is also the source and seed of all energies, trees, forests and winds.
Be aware of the life air, fresh and serene flowing from the forest groves into the heart. The heartbeat is noticeably slower and finer, the air cleanses the energy channels and the purity of the forest gives protection to all impurities.

Honour and respect this magnificent place, and strength, protection and peace shall be present immediately. Trees have been sheltering humans forever and still give presence, balance and protection. Whenever there is no way out, in daily life or meditation, just think about the forest and take (an imaginative) stroll around the groves of ancient forests. Be aware of the sounds, smells and presently, be aware of the heartbeat. Feel the tranquillity and shelter.

Trees are the great guardians of this earth and we have been guest for long enough to know that the elements are our friends. Likewise, the waters, which are gently flowing along the groves to nurture the land and animals. This beautiful place also holds flowers and herbs which are aromatic and lushly spread across the grove.

Breathe, and be aware that finding shelter is necessary, one can submit and see that life is always depending. The trees are creating the oxygen we need, and the other way around, the trees are absorbing the carbon dioxide of our lungs to transform it into oxygen. Naturally, the trees have been feeding us with oxygen, since life existed, and one can be eternally thankful.

Give thanks and appreciation to the forest grove, where a beautiful river flows, and where birds are singing a sweet song.

Just be humble and steady as a tree and life will flower.

Once upon a time, there lived the oldest and wisest trees in the world. These trees were so rooted, that no one could shake them, as these trees were holding onto the ground, no one could ever rip them out, no giant, no dragon, no king, nor queen, but they all know, the wonderful humbleness of a tree.
So humble and kind, the tree doesn't care, about all this, the tree is not winning any prize, but the honour and respect of all humankind. Even the wind, sometimes tries, but hardly comes to terms with this forest kingdom, where the trees hold onto their roots.

So find a comfortable position and imagine your spine. You see the spine, vertebrae for vertebrae and there is also a root, imagine, the root coming from the lowest bottom of the spine and spreading throughout the soil, into the layers of the ground. That ground then is the fundament for our balance.

So we breathe and breathe in the balance. Equally in and out, Balanced breath, equally in and out.

All in harmony and balance, the breathing flows naturally and the body is aligned with all the elements. As the spine is straight, we are relaxing our jaw and head. We can let go of any tension, to relax and ease, into a smile.

Breathe and smile, gently.
Breathe and be in balance.
Like the roots of a tree, we find steadiness in the ground.
And we can also tone a sound, that helps us to relax.

Let's open our mouth, wide and full, on AHHH, hold the sound as long as possible. AHHHH
Now breathe again and find the balance and harmony, in the ground, and of course, we can tone another sound.

This time for our heart, the Sound goes UHHHH, very mild and long, we can tone this once more, UUHHHH and there you connect to your heart and now let's embrace the smile, let's connect to our head with HUMMMM, long and gently, sound HUMMMMM. These three sounds, AHHH, UHHH, HUMMM are the essential building blocks of life.

Like a tree has a seed, that's the AAH, it also has a stem, that's the UHH, and of course, it has a crown and that's the HUMMM. All together these three sounds AUM give the primal sound, a wonderful attraction.

Sometimes, a lot of flowers are coming from a tree, sometimes, the tree dances in the wind to find expression, and sometimes the fruits of a tree are growing from just a little seed.

One seed has all the information a tree needs to live on for thousands of years, and even in the nights, the trees are growing upwards and downwards, isn't that interesting?
As all the beings, like the trees, are part of this world, we are also growing in the night, yet, we have to be sure, that we are relaxed and ready for the upcoming night. Therefore the trees prepared a nice soothing song for the upcoming good night.
It is again, around that time, where everything sets, from the shine, of the sun, to the son, of a kingdom divine. Please, enjoy the moment, and breathe, like we are here together to live.

Enjoy the moment and breathe, The air comes in and out, there is so much doubt,
But leave it all behind,
Be sure and one shall find,
That there is more to the dark,
That there is always a spark,
That ignites the wisdom of life.
Even though we respect the light,
We know, it must be night, Whenever we are in sight,
we arrange to be alright,
With a song, that goes all night long.
Sing it and feel it in the breath.
Sing it and feel it in the air,
Breathe and be enjoying the now. Everything is in care, just trust, just trust. There is no more, do's or must.

Just relax and keep the breath, Feel the peace and the ease.

Root yourself to the ground,
And hear the beautiful sound.

It is the air, in the space,
Now imagine a face,
Let it be kind and smile,
Hold it on for a while,
Enjoy the sight,
attracting the night

A moment we listen to the trees, we are also listening to our selves, conscious and wise, we are all rooted on the same earth.
Be kind and bring your friends, to this wonderful kingdom of peace and harmony. Enjoy every bit of it.

Trust Meditation

Bring yourself to ease and breathe. Do you feel your tippy toes? Breathe and relax, there is awareness, so energy in the little toe, the first toe, the second toe, the third toe and the fourth toe. Do you see and feel? Be aware, that energy is now filling the space in your feet and breathing makes it happen.

Breathe and feel again, your toes are alive and relaxed. Now feel your whole feet- Be aware of the energy at the feet. Be aware of the ankle and of the whole leg. Now of the thigh, the root of the spine and the whole spine. Breathe and feel into the body, now your whole lower body is relaxed and filled with awareness. Sense the trust and the security, be aware of the belly and now imagine you find shelter in a deep, deep cave made of rose crystals.

Imagine walking into this crystal cave of light and glowing crystal quartz in rose. One can see the reflection and the beautiful splendor of the rose, it is a whole cave with nice rose colored walls, all surrounding you.
One finds a place in the crystal cave to sense the stability and protection. Just trust and feel safe.
The whole of your body is in union with the awareness and we start to be breathing slower and slower, we are becoming finer and finer and with every breath we are becoming lighter and lighter. Our whole upper body is now filled with peaceful and radiant light.

From the belly it radiates to all the parts of the body. The chest is filled with awareness and we feel the chest. There is a room, where we meet our friend, and kindly greet our friend with a smile. Smile and feel the friendship eternally from the heart.

The whole heart and the upper body are now illuminated with the light of friendship.

Just breathe and feel the sensations coming and going, sense the air and know every storm also might pass. The air comes and goes again. All is coming and going, but we are here, right now in safety and peace. Now relax your head with the light of peace. Peace be with every part of the head and jaw. All is illuminated in peaceful light of relaxation.

The whole head relaxes and we find absolute serenity in the breath. Breathing equally in and out, all is in care, all is fine and we find the ease.

The Storm is outside and is now noticeable as the two boys thank each other and the teacher for the serenity.

Let's together speak a prayer for the kingdom and for the whole world.

May all beings in this kingdom and the whole world be happy and at peace.
May all beings be at peace and happy.

May we all find absolute serenity.
May there be trust and happiness all around, May we find the inner voice that guides us, Towards peace, love and unity.

Trust starts with trusting one self. This trust to oneself comes from the knowledge who we are and what really is. With meditation, says the teacher, we can learn how life really is.

Find a comfortable seat, bringing your whole body into balance between earth and sky. You can sit or lay on the ground in a comfortable place. Watch your breath coming equally in and out. Working with the breath is the one fundamental trust, as we live, we breathe.
Come to terms with your body, come to ease, settle, there is nothing to fear, relax, with a voice that is guiding you into meditation.
Just trust the breathing as it is coming and going, gently notice the breath and be aware of the sensation of the breath entering the nostrils and leaving them again.
Equally in and out again, breathe and be aware of how it comes into your nose tip, into your body and your heart. Here in the heart, the breath is home. The beloved invites the lover and everything comes home. One can notice there is awareness in the breath which is bringing us home into the body and the heart.

We notice every part of the body, from the heart to the belly, to the spine, to the shoulders and head, and even to the tippy toes. Feel how the heart is opening and the chest is widening. Here in the heart is where the eternal spark of light resides.
Breathe out all you are letting go of and receive all you breathe in. One can make up a thought, we are letting go, and we can make up a thought that we receive, therefore we can inhale I Am Trust, and exhale all that we are not. Breathe, in I am Trust and breathe out again. Continue and know that the thought and words travel with the breath, into your heart.
Find peace and relax the body, coming to a state of trust and harmony.
With every single breath, one is becoming lighter and lighter. 'I am Light' travels with the breath and comes into every cell of the body. The whole body is now very light and even so light it starts to float and lifting of the ground, just with the help of the breath.
The body is so light and trusting the body floats into the space of Trust, the whole body is now fully in a space of trust and peace. Feel the ease, the small breeze from the air entering the nose and coming to the heart.
In our imagination we can see a nice tender space where we can land again for good care, like in a flower field, full of moss and soft ground, landing there it feels like we are home in a space of trust and balance.
Feel the balance of the breath, equally inhaling and exhaling, as the thoughts arise we can just notice them like we notice the leaves dancing in the wind.
See the beautiful wind playing with the trees, also these trees are giving us shelter and equanimity, just trust and find a nice space close to that tree.
The trees are holding up the earth and likewise, we can hold trust within us, just steady and always growing up towards the sky.
Embrace nature and feel the rhythm of the breath, find the heart and maybe there is a friend who likes to join us. Do you have a friend you like to play with? Invite this friend with a smile into the garden within the heart.

This friend is appearing with also a smile greeting us dearly and giving us a glance of gratitude and compassion. Trust is our friend and we have the happy community of someone who knows the way.
Let's sit and listen to the spring source that is coming down the stream, the subtle element makes us clear and the friend smiles again.

To trust means to have full faith in goodness in personality.

Whatever will be, everything turns out just for a reason. Therefore always be thankful and happy for all the little things. Even watch the flowers who are so happily growing on the field providing nectar for the bees, and see the trees?
Do they ever complain? Still and steady they hold on for days and days on end, especially when there is a good friend. Walking along the small stream, the water is crystal clear and there is a fish or two within the river that flows into the lake of consciousness.

One can sit on the lake and watch the eagle birds glide and hover for good. Effortless the wind is holding them in space and every face is enjoying the fresh breeze, nothing better than this.

The eagle glides in a circular motion upwards without any flaps and the beauty of the moment seems to last forever, light and kind, the trust is in the air, who else should care?

There is the lovely friend, the family, or maybe the brother or sister and when everyone you know comes together, then it is time for a nice festivity.
On the lake, there is much to see, as some great mountains are erected on the vast horizon giving us a glimpse of majesty, the royal throne of the earth's surface, and up above there thrones the sun within the space.
All elements give a nice picture and the community plays music, or just enjoys the peaceful, trusting moment of harmony and whenever there is a light there can be equanimity.
Finding a reflection in the lake, one can see a mirror face of the wonderful surface, within this endless space.
Holding the moment of trust, even when there is no doubt, no lack and desire to be somewhere else, that is balance and trust.

Giving a hand to someone, and see there is a smile that illuminates the world, that is trust. Even together or just being alone, that is trust. Know to be content even when there is a surprising event, like a dancing tree.

Without any fault, everything finds a place on this earthly surface, even the rain. All come the same, yet we trust and have everything we need. A shelter is right there. But behold, there is a light within the hut, there might be someone in there. All in care, just trust and see, everything is in divine harmony.
'Knock, knock someone there?' The door opens and it is our favourite teacher, simply waving with a hand, smiling and inviting into his land. A shelter of hope and peace, just trust and feel the ease.

Warm and cosy it shall be, yes there is a certain equanimity. A stove heats the water for tea and the smell of wood is right with thee. How come we are also all living this dream collectively?
Life is miraculous and wonderful as sometimes unexplainably we just trust and see the magic unfold within the matter of the now, breathing and opening our hearts for the chance of goodness, one shall receive the mercy of the light.
' I have no fright, as I know it is forever and alright. Life as it is, the spirit shall go on and on.'

The tea boils and one can maybe feel a little of that spirit of life, being timeless and eternal, forever lasting like the connecting of the friends and family. Whatever shall be, shall be.

In the future we trust in Peace, Love and Unity, knowing everything is in divine harmony. Breathe equally.

Notice the subtle sensation of the thoughts and the breath coming to terms with the light, knowing everything shall be alright. The perfect harmony is here, within the heart of everyone.

The flowers and the trees, the friends and families all together like to live in harmonies. All are the same in their goal to come back home.

Where the heart is there is bliss, and all longing to never miss a chance of meeting someone new, just trust and what we will do? Smile and breathe, greet as a friend always and forever one to be.
Then, all shall be happy.

Within the whole body, there is now the light of trust spreading and we can know that all living entities are seeking the same light of trust, and trust is everywhere and there and within the heart. Like there is air within the space there is love for all in the face of a smiling heart.
We are all a part of this world. Even when the sun sets for a goodbye it shall still shine, let's embrace the stillness of the lake one more time and see the setting suns face shining for a good night over the hills and within the heart, all we are a part.

This space is here and now for us to feel, from the tippy-toes to the head, to the chest and all around the nose, with the jaw and around the neck, the arms, shoulders and hands are relaxed, as well as the fingertips and the lips, the jaw and the neck.
The whole body is filled with lightness and trust, as we breathe there is no must, but we can do, whatever there is to do! We can also trust! Where there is no must, just let be, and feel free to also renounce and come back home to the premises of the body where the soul finds its heart.
There, everything is a start and we begin to breathe.

Be aware of the breath and let it flow naturally, just be aware of the body and relax from the head to the toes. The sunshine is now all gone, yet one can see the reflection within the sky, that is coming in beautiful colours and o 'wonder why we deserve to be blessed. Of course, because we trust.
Let's adjust the body to find a comfortable way, of trusting our close ones every day, maybe invite them for a dream with the heart-full space of trust, giving oneself to the best.

Give thanks and appreciation to the best ones close by, and be grateful for every single breath, as it comes naturally, we give thanks to nature accordingly.
All the appreciation to the world family.
May all beings be happy and live in equanimity.
Now, close the eyes and see yourself, just sitting in a nice tranquil state of equilibrium. This beautiful light of love surrounds you, and here you can take shelter, with all the joy and gratitude.
Maybe now, you can see yourself from head to toe, from toe to head, and again from head to toe. Nice light surrounds you and helps you to grow.

As the sun shines we all need light to grow, for a moment we can see our friends and family within this world. With light and growth. Smile and greet all the known faces.
Be aware again of the heart and be aware of the breath. This is your shelter, and only you know the truth within your heart, so does every person know the truth within their hearts.
Let the truth shine, and just relax, as a smooth chant can help purify and prepare for the night.
I am the Light of the World,
I am the Light of the World,
I am, I am, I am the Light of the World.
You are the Light of the World,
You are the Light of the World,
You are, you are, you are the Light of the World.
We are the Light of the World,
We are the Light of the World,
We are, we are, we are the Light of the World.
Be happy and smile

Imagine there is a light, a beautiful light, that shines from within
your heart. It is so bright and beautiful, it's around your whole body.
Breathe and feel the lightness throughout the whole body. See that light expanding with every breath. In and out, the breathing is equal and natural, the light expands and surrounds even the aura around you.
From within your heart there shines the source of this light and with every breath, we illuminate our whole body, from the head, one can see the head glowing in a beautiful protective light, to the feet. With every breath, the light travels throughout the body.
We start from the crown of our head, there is a light slowly sinking into the face. We breathe and with every breath, the light sinks lower and lower into the area of the eyes. Our eyes and all the muscles around the eyes are illuminated with protective, healing light.

Just focus on the breathing and let the light sink into the ears, the cheeks and the jaw. All the little tissues and membranes are equally illuminated, around the nose, on the jaw, and inside of the head, where the nose meets the mouth. We focus on this point, where the nose meets the mouth and sense our breathing. We can even hear the breath coming in and going out again. It is a constant stream of energy that comes with the air, and the sound is clear and soothing.
One can find comfort in the sound of the breath and know there is a light, a life protection from within and around us.
The Life Breath is everyone's mandatory need and we can connect with this friend our whole life. It is always there for us. Let's breathe again and feel how mandatory and friendly the life air is.

See the focus where the nose and mouth meet. and sense the air coming into the nostrils and going out again. It is a constant Hello, Breath. Goodbye Breath. Always and ever coming and going. We are just witnessing this process, this endless stream and ensure everything is smooth and equal.
Equally in and out again, the protective light shines within our whole head and a feeling of peace and protection spreads around the face. We can smile and ease into the breath. Maybe sigh or yawn, whatever feels now fine with you.
Also note any sensation, whatever it is, warmth, cold, vibrating, tickling, throbbing, pulsing, any sensation is possible, and whatever comes, we keep on breathing.
We see the breath travelling into our nostrils and down the throat into the lungs. From our head and our heart the protective light also illuminates the throat and neck area.

Along the spine, the protective light shines in every cell from the head, to the throat, to the middle of the body.

Here the light sinks further down with the breath and we include as many parts as possible, like the shoulders and arms, elbows, wrists and hands.

All are surrounded by protective light. We can open our hands to the sky and see how the light illuminates now every cell, even the fingertips.

Let's put our hands into our middle, onto the belly and feel into the body. Protective light is spreading from the hands and the heart into the belly and around the whole lower body.

The healing light of protection expands and brings peace and ease.
We breathe and with every breath, the light sinks further down the spine, from the belly to the hips, into the root of the spine.

Here we relax and find that the healing light of protection is welcome to also illuminate our thighs, knees, legs, ankles and feet. The healing light of protection even shines into the smallest parts of the tippy toes and brings peace and relaxation.

From the tippy toes we can come upwards, according to our breath we can travel with the awareness, the light of protection up the legs, to the bottom of the spine and again, slowly up the spine to the heart. Here, in the heart, we hold this healing light of protection and let it blossom like a flower.

With every breath, each pedal of this wonderful flower of light expands from the heart and shines throughout the whole body.

The whole flower of light is now really beautiful and blossoming. We can imagine we are meeting a friend, and we can bring this flower as a present to the heart of this friend.

Let's smile and innerly say: Here, this is the light of my heart, may it protect and bring you peace.

You can repeat this prayer and see your friend kindly accepting it.
Here, this is the flower of my heart, may it protect and bring you peace.
Here, this is the flower of my heart, may it protect and bring you peace.

Here, this is the flower of my heart, may it protect and bring you peace.

By saying this we give meaning to the flower and the light, therefore one knows what this light intends to do.

Protection and Peace is now upon us and we can see the whole body of ours and our friend be illuminated.
By breathing we uphold the light, by breathing we maintain the luminosity.

Whenever we are in a hurry, we can also call this protective light and ask for a healing light of protection. Please Light, Protect me, and give me shelter of Peace.

The healing light is like the breathing always with us, when we are aware of it, it comes into presence.

In our imagination let's wander around our home and in the garden to maintain this healing light. Just breathe and feel the connection to the sunlight.
See how the light of protection and the sunlight are the same.
See the trees and the grass, and know all this is grown from the sunlight, one with the light of protection.

See the sky and the endless horizon and know, your inner voice can always call for the light of protection.

May All beings be in protection and Peace, May All find relaxation and ease.

May All have a life of light and love. May All live in Peace and Harmony, May All join the Unity.

This attractive light can bring us from the unsafe shores of darkness to the beautiful shores of the light kingdom.

Find yourself comfortable and relaxed, you are now safe and in protection.

Affirmations:

Affirmation & Prayer for Attraction
Prayer has since worked and relieved people. Shamans, nature man, from all over the world have attracted wonders and forces to helped the tribe, like in the Mongolian desert, a Shaman sang with his tribe for relief. Rituals of dance and sacrifice were done. However, eventually, the Shaman fell into deep wishful prayer, finally attracting the rain.
Same stories are heard from all over the world. Deep, intentional prayer can send out a message of change, and actually transform a circumstance immediately. Like Sebastian was looking into the Sky

and the clouds were just making space for some sunshine. Did he pray for it? Maybe.
Let's affirm and trust in the words, which shall attract all good things. Notably, all activities towards speaking, singing and praying are auspicious when used consciously and with humility.
Writing is a wonderful base of speaking, praying or reciting, therefore it deserves a special thanks. Giving it a proper place, writing will be discussed in later sections about attractive actions.
Attractive words include words that are full of worth and value. Praise, Glorification, Personal Truth, even abstract thoughts and ideas hold value. Words of highest order, are attracting pure results like love, bliss and joy.
'Today, I shall not worry, just for now, I shall be happy.'
' Just now, you shall be joyful, happy and at peace!'
'May all living beings be happy.'
Very mellow and subtle, these affirmations actually work wonders. Happiness and joy can be so easily attracted, especially in times of grief, anger, frustration, pain, and so on. Love functions through the space- time and is a universal force, stronger than any other force. Likewise, it emanates from within the heart and radiates. Therefore, try it out. Speak it and feel. Loud, or soft. Play with it.
Most importantly: Mean it. Truthfully.
Praising a loved one is also giving results very easily.
'You have done this very nicely!' 'Well done!'

' We are a good team!'

Positivity can uplift everyone to a mood swing, giving the truth with love and compassionate holds endless value. Truth spoken without compassionate has no effect. Therefore, affirm it and mean it. Practice it, and be aware of voice, tone, and body language. Feel it and play with it.
To glorify is a good tool to enchant a personality that is worth of glorification. In most religions God is glorified, in natural tribes the weather entities are glorified, in simple means, one can even glorify ones cooking gear. Actually, in India there is one day in the year where all the utensils, from plates, to tables, to other things are glorified. This is to show respect for their service.

' O my beloved tea cup, I behold you to truly nurture me with kindness and a relief from today's stress.'
'O beloved rain clouds, I glorify the water you give us, so the crops can grow into a fruitful harvest.'
'Dear loved one, just one glance at your glorious form creates a smile of peace within my heart.'
Like this, one can practice this and really embrace the feeling, full of love and devotion. Really, life is emotional, life is fluid and ecstatic, however we live it. Say these words even to yourself. Making clear, appreciation attracts self- confidence.
'I am the Light of the World, You are the Light of the World, We are the Light of the World.'

Sing it, dance to it, be like an over-confident child, that is somewhat proud and boasting of energy. It gives strength and power.

Have you ever seen the sports team of New Zealand's rugby team? It's a rough sport, but before every match, the team dances the tribal glorification of nature. This energized confidence is put to use for greater team efforts. Affirmations also work on the personal level, speaking truth about and personally to oneself.

'I feel…'

'I want to attract…'

'I am happy as I am, or even so, unhappiness cannot limit me.'

Let it be personal and stress your individuality, knowing to be part of the whole. We are all unique, yet different. This is the basic and personal truth of behaviour and philosophy.

Directly, one can also boost confidence, compassion, peace, and relationships by wording affirmations according to ones needs.

'Today, I speak truly and attract truth.'

'Now, I shall find happiness and attract happiness around me.'

'Let there be peace in every word I say.'

'May I trust the people around me, with compassion and kindness.'

'May I trust in the Law of Attraction, Light and Love.'

The universal force of Love is all-pervading like a constant, yet fine element, like the sky, love is everywhere, pervading everything. Trust in it. It is all-good.

Joyful affirmations

This is a mantra meditation. The joyful affirmations can be repeated silently in your head or spoken out loud. Try to really connect with the meaning behind the words.

May All the Joy be with All
May all the love be with all
May all the happiness be with all
Love, Peace & Harmony
May all the Joy be with Us
May all the love be with Us
May all the happiness be with us.
Love, Peace & Harmony
May all the Joy be with You
May all the Love be with you
May all the happiness be with you
Love, Peace & Harmony
May all the Joy be with me
May all the love be with me
May all the happiness be with me
Love, Peace & Harmony

I am the Joy of the World
I am the joy of the world
I am I am I am the joy of the world

You are the joy of the world
You are the joy of the world
You are, you are, you are the joy of the world

We are the joy of the world
We are the joy of the world
We are, we are, we are, the joy of the world.

Love, Joy and Harmony
Peace in Unity
Satisfaction
Love Attraction
Joy and Harmony,
Peace in Unity
Satisfaction

Affirming with Mantra:

Mantra is a special form of affirmation and meditation. It comes from the word manas meaning 'the mind' and tra meaning 'a tool to still or pacify'. One can receive a Mantra through a teacher or discipleship, receiving with it the full potential of the source or sacred sounds.

Mantra is also sung or recited. Like a motto or slogan, one can truly feel the intensity through repetition. There are special mantras like the Maha-mantra. The great teacher of meditation Srila Prabhupada gives a purport on the MAHA-Mantra:

The transcendental vibration established by the chanting of Hare Krsna, Hare Krsna, Krsna Krsna, Hare Hare/ Hare Rama, Hare Rama, Rama Rama, Hare Hare is the sublime method of reviving our Krsna consciousness. As living spiritual souls we are all originally Krsna conscious entities, but due to our association with matter from time immemorial, our consciousness is now polluted by the material atmosphere

. The material atmosphere, in which we are now living, is called maya, or illusion. Maya means "that which is not." And what is this illusion? The illusion is that we are all trying to be lords of material nature, while actually we are under the grip of her stringent laws. When a servant artificially tries to imitate the all-powerful master, this is called illusion. In this polluted concept of life, we are all trying to exploit the resources of material nature, but actually we are becoming more and more entangled in her complexities. Therefore, although we are engaged in a hard struggle to conquer nature, we are ever more dependent on her.

This illusory struggle against material nature can be stopped at once by revival of our Krsna consciousness. Krsna consciousness is not an artificial imposition on the mind; this consciousness is the original energy of the living entity. When we hear the transcendental vibration, this consciousness is revived. And this process is recommended for this age by authorities. By practical experience also, one can perceive that by chanting this maha-mantra, or the Great Chanting for Deliverance, one can at once feel a transcendental ecstasy coming through from the spiritual stratum. And when one is factually on the plane of spiritual understanding—surpassing the stages of senses, mind, and intelligence—one is situated on the transcendental plane. This chanting of Hare Krsna, Hare Krsna, Krsna Krsna, Hare Hare/ Hare Rama, Hare Rama, Rama Rama, Hare Hare is directly enacted from the spiritual platform, and thus this sound vibration surpasses all lower strata of consciousness—namely sensual, mental, and intellectual.

There is no need, therefore, to understand the language of the mantra, nor is there any need for mental speculation or any intellectual adjustment for chanting this maha-mantra. It springs automatically from the spiritual platform, and as such, anyone can take part in the chanting without any previous qualification, and dance in ecstasy. We have seen this practically.
Even a child can take part in the chanting, or even a dog can take part in it. Of course, for one who is too entangled in material life, it takes a little more time to come to the standard point, but even such a materially engrossed man is raised to the spiritual platform very quickly. When the mantra is chanted by a pure devotee of the Lord in love, it has the greatest efficacy on the hearers, and as such, this chanting should be heard from the lips of a pure devotee of the Lord, so that immediate effects can be achieved.

As far as possible, chanting from the lips of nondevotees should be avoided. Milk touched by the lips of a serpent has poisonous effects. The word Hara is the form of addressing the energy of the Lord, and the words Krsna and Rama are forms of addressing the Lord Himself. Both Krsna and Rama mean "the supreme pleasure," and Hara is the supreme pleasure energy of the Lord, changed to Hare in the vocative. The supreme pleasure energy of the Lord helps us to reach the Lord. The material energy, called maya, is also one of the multienergies of the Lord. And we, the living entities, are also the energy—marginal energy—of the Lord. The living entities are described as superior to material energy. When the superior energy is in contact with the inferior energy, an incompatible situation arises; but when the superior marginal energy is in contact with the superior energy, called Hara, the living entity is established in his happy, normal condition.

These three words, namely Hare, Krsna, and Rama, are the transcendental seeds of the maha-mantra. The chanting is a spiritual call for the Lord and His internal energy, Hara, to give protection to the conditioned soul. This chanting is exactly like the genuine cry of a child for its mother. Mother Hara helps the devotee achieve the grace of the supreme father, Hari, or Krsna, and the Lord reveals Himself to the devotee who chants this mantra sincerely. No other means of spiritual realization, therefore, is as effective in this age as chanting the maha-mantra: Hare Krsna, Hare Krsna, Krsna Krsna, Hare Hare/ Hare Rama, Hare Rama, Rama Rama, Hare Hare.

This Mantra can be repeated and practiced by chanting it on beads, between ring-finger and thumb holding one bead at a time and consciously repeating Hare Krsna Hare Krsna Krsna Krsna Hare Hare Hare Rama Hare Rama Rama Rama Hare Hare.

This affirmation can be translated as follows:

'O divine energy,
Supplier of everything,
Source of Joy and Happiness.'

'O dear friend,
How can I serve you?'
'Most wonderful beloved, how can I make you happy?'
'Wonderful life, how can I live fully?'

'Please dear Friend, show your smile.'

All these affirmations use a question, inquiry and bid to form a desire to know and to address.
Affirmations are only fully potent when addressing a personality with a certain mood of honest relation.

There are five great types of reference or relationship, namely neutral, servitorship, friendly, parental and conjugal. All these have one thing in common: It is always a relation from person to person, from personality to personality.

No toaster or car should be praised or asked for, without including a personality. This aspect makes everything a personal trait, like:

'Please let this kitchen be clean! For
My friend, parent, children or spouse.'

See, there is always personality involved, therefore, to activate an affirmation one should address a person directly.
The Maha-Mantra is the address to the Original Personality and Supreme Personality.

Be aware of the mood you are sitting in, be present and prepare the affirmations carefully. Light a candle and maybe erect an altar that helps to focus the intention unto the desired outcome, for example:

A beautiful altar is filled with precious gems for protection and images of loved-ones. One can now affirm;

May all beings be protected and safe,
May my family be healthy and happy,
May I be healthy and happy.

I can take care of myself and of my family,
I can help the world by being myself, in goodness.
I trust a better world to be, in happiness and unity.

I am safe and sound, You are safe and sound, We are safe and sound. Let us breathe and unite in peace.
Let us give thanks and gratitude to every breath.

May we all be aware that life is a miracle,
May you see the beauty within,
And may I connect to the highest Truth.

The focus is most dominant guardian for any endeavour. Therefore, to remain focused and balance one needs a proper space and community. The right, meditative space will allow miracles to happen; as a seeing goes:

One can only grow as great as ones surrounding.

For example, no Giant Mammoth tree can grow in the dense jungle, only in a grove where there is proper space and circumstance, by time, the tree can unfold as a giant.

Universal Affirmation

Sit peacefully, relaxed and in a meditative space of tranquillity. Be prepared for sound, so find a comfortable seat or lay down flat. In both ways, when meditating face North and open the palms to the sky.

This hand gesture means 'openness', or
'ready to receive'.

Now use breath to calm down the mind and continue with equal breathing for a few deep moments. Let the inhale and exhale be equal and focus on the heart.
Notice the constant stream of air flowing along the nose tip, in and out it goes. Very equally and rhythmic. Body, spine, emotions and mind are in alignment and balance.

Feel the ground, either on the buttocks or with the whole body. Be aware of the whole body as a unit. This wholeness starts within the heart. Focus here and breathe equally, with an equanimous mind.

Whatever thoughts arise, be aware and let them pass. Don't worry, like ebb and flood, thoughts arise and fade naturally. Just observe this phenomenon and keep balance.

Balance is everything. In a Space, to create balance, one can utter the syllable AUM. This word (☐) or Omkara is the whole manifestation of the All-attractive Supreme Personality.

When we utter this sound, the whole body vibrates in a natural frequency. Simultaneously, it is a greeting to address the Supreme Reservoir of all things and worlds.

This divine sound is very simple, yet ultimately profound. One can hear this resonance everywhere in nature, for example in the rivers or even within the breath. Be aware of the sound of the breath and just listen for some equal breaths.

Breath, equally in and equally out again. Be aware of the sound and let it sink into the heart space.

Here is the centre of Attraction and one can witness how the whole body is maintained from here. Let the sound of the breath evenly sink into the belly and to the feet.

Be aware of the sensations and remain in balance.

Now, one can utter the sound. The mouth is fully open to start uttering the Aaaahh, as long as possible. This sound A vibrates within the abdomen or more specifically within the area of the navel. This is the sound of creation.
Now, you can utter the sound U, nice and long. Keep it, maintain and feel it. This sound vibrates within the heart space, straight up the spine, and it is the manifestation of Unity and connection.
Now, you can utter the sound Mmm. The mouth is completely closed and it vibrates in the area of the throat. Keep it inside and let it sound, even up to the crown of your head. The whole jaw, skull, neck and shoulders are addressed with this sound of purity.
So, A-U-M are three individual sounds, in a connected flow of sound. This is pure, creative energy which addresses the Supreme reservoir of all Attraction.

Sound and Tone: AaaaUuuuMmm. Feel it, vibrate with it and let it free naturally.

Practice makes perfect. Repeat and rehearse. This sound is to create space and purify existence. It addresses also the lake of consciousness just on the feet of the Supreme Attractor whose eyes are like the sun and moon.

So let's speak to the heart's content, addressing the Supreme Attractor in person, one can utter this sacred sound which acts as a spiritual key for tuning in and saying Hello.

Of course, the Supreme Personality is always very nice to devotees who are thus addressing his abode and Reservoir of all pleasure:

Om (A-U-M), O highest person, please accept my humble request, I am here to learn how to attract...
May this meditation lead to Your Reservoir of abundance, pleasantness and attraction.

Thus, the highest person who sits within our hearts knows what is our desire and can listen.

When, in meditation, one shall know what to attract: Let's say, 'One wants to attract... a pure and healthy life', or '...a good way to learn for my exam. 'one can easily say it. From the heart, everything is accepted. Just be humble and utter your wishes internally, externally, or write it down.

We shall for now envision internally, but we will come back to external, and contemplative methods like writing.

Just imagine why you came here. What is the purpose of your visit?

Like a messenger comes to the King and reports news or proposes an inquiry, one can be inquisitive and ask for anything. The Supreme Reservoir in person understands and is always open to granting a conversation or even permission.

Good things, prescribed in scriptures, like purity or the search for the absolute Truth are always welcome.

This Truth is essentially within everyone's heart and thus one carries it around everywhere.

Meditation means also internal contemplation. Therefore, help yourself with enough time and space. Five-minute meditations fill a gap or can be integrated before a meal, proper sit, breathe and meditate. Meditation can thus make every life circumstance a conscious effort for attraction and well-being. Meditation creates space, like with a Mantra (Om), and within this space, one can attract anything. Be patient and listen. Enough space for meditation is necessary to feel attraction and abundance holistically.

Light Mantra Affirmation

There is a Mantra, an affirmation, on how to still the mind, and create good vibrations. It goes like this:

I am the Light of the World,
I am the Light of the World,
I am, I am, I am the Light of the World.

You are the Light of the world,
You are the Light of the World,
You are, You are, You are the Light of the World.

We are the Light of the World,
We are the Light of the World,
We are, We are, We are the Light of the World.

Light is life. Light is love.
Light is everything around.

With every light, one can blink and address the eyes, the receivers of light.

Blink and let the eyes shine. Smile and give thanks for the light.

With steady practice of this Mantra, one can still the mind and attract light in dark times.
Light can be interchanged with everything that makes life liveable, like:

I am the Love of the World,
You are the Love of the World,
We are the Love of the World.

I am the Peace of the World,
You are the Peace of the World,
We are the Peace of the World.

I am the Unity of the World,
You are the Unity of the World,
We are the Unity of the World.

Or speak an affirmation of goodness, purity and blessing.

I am attracting Goodness now and forever,
You are attracting Goodness within time,
We are attracting Goodness evermore.

Let purity bring Me closer to myself,
Let purity bring Us closer together,
Let purity bring Them closer to themselves

May all beings be blessed,
May the world, time and circumstance be blessed.
Affirmation work effectively through devotion and repetition, therefore repeat these phrases in perfect alignment. Feel the purpose and need for the affirmation knowing that words attract, whatever we say.

In regards to sacred Mantras like AUM and Affirmation, it is most common to create a mood of prayer including honesty and compassion.

Thank you for this light, thank you to shine bright
Thanks for all the love from the sky above.
Thankfulness, Truth and Compassionate Love.

Sitting upright and align to sky and earth, being grounded and free to speak is the basis of every good meditation.

To create a meditative place one can speak the following formulas, to purify a meditation room:

May this space be clean and free of envy, anger and other things,
May this place serve for meditation and affirmation.
May I find a comfortable seat.

To speak honestly means also to speak in full understanding of the purpose. Why Am I here? To meditate, ok. Let the room know, light a candle or incense and find your own space of tranquillity.

Create an oasis of abundance within the heart, as well as within the living space. Practically, every space can be transformed into a meditative space.

Everybody is a temple and everyone is living in their temple.

One who knows about the sanctity of a space can still the lake of consciousness easily. Thus, wishes and desires are reflected perfectly and the ground can be visible.

From the ground sometimes unconscious or stored attractions are coming to the surface. Like a habit, a thought pattern, or a simple word. These can be fetched, transformed and used with the matter of the breath and consciousness. Everything in life has a reason, a ground to exist.

It is a balance about moving and being, speaking and receiving. Prepare a well-balanced place, safely and protected, in a sacred setting of peace and tranquility. This may be the soil for good growth.

Give thanks to the heart, the spiritual heart where sweet Balance resides. This focus can be a gaze that is shifted within, towards the heart, or easier to the middle of the face, on the nose-tip. A candle light helps to focus this attention.

See a nice candle flickering on this altar and continue meditating, in silence, to cleanse the space.
Affirm safety and protection, trust and happiness.
'With every word I affirm that this space is sacred and spiritual, safe and peaceful.
May peace and protection surround this place for the whole while.
May I trust in the higher good for all.'

Affirm in mind, word or even writing.

'I am the Light of the World,
I am the Light of the World,
I am, I am, I am the Light of the World.'

'You are the Light of the World.
You are the Light of the World,
You are, you are, you are the Light of World.'

'We are the Light of the World.
We are the Light of the World,
We are, we are, we are the Light of the World.'

Put your palms on your heart and breathe equally. Relax and let the affirmation sink in.
Be aware of the subtle vibration of sound and harmony within the heart. Feel the pulse and notice that light and lightness is filling your heart.

Light is essential, so is the identification with a certain aspect of life. Life is light, therefore it resounds everywhere. Light is the great base of all life and connector of all living beings.

Appreciate the heart, the light and personality. Personality expresses itself through (per) sound (sonar). Personality is the light within every movement, thought and character. It is the essence of all life. Life itself has character and it is light, full of wisdom, eternal and blissful.

Life is intelligent and we can make life a good friend, as we speak nice words and craft pleasant thoughts. For every circumstance there are affirmations, for example when a loved-one is not well, or when trust is lacking, or when we ask for forgiveness, or before a supper.

With patience and understanding one can turn life into a prayerful affirmation of goodness and grace.

A life in harmony is thus attainable through sacred sound vibration and affirmation.

<u>Waking up with affirmations:</u>

May this day be fulfilled with light and joy,
 May I give thanks to nature, the earth and sky,
to family and friends, and all living beings.
May all beings be light-hearted and happy, joyful at peace.
I find success and ease within every breeze.
May the life air help me to relief.
I breathe happiness and joy.

To confirm your inner Truth, wake up with these prayers:

I affirm and encourage others, as I do myself.
I alone hold the truth of who I am.

Bring affirmations into daily life and see how a mindset can make a good morning.

Before dressing you can speak following affirmations:

I am beautiful and I can see the beauty in others. My heart is full of grace and pleasure.
I shall attract goodness with who I am. I am who I am.

I am wearing a mindset of peace and unity, I am wearing this for my beloved friends, family, workmates or surrounding. I just want to be beautiful. May all I do and wear be a sign of inner trust and truth.

Dresses make people, a saying goes, but it is really the mindset and focus that can attract people and goodness. A dress does make a difference, subtle, but noticeable it is the consciousness behind all we do and focus how we act. Clean and natural clothing are an expression of ones mood, therefore be aware of how you dress your inner state of consciousness. Basically, clothing means protection. Protection from the cold, the heat, the sun, or the glances of others. Keep in mind, that affirmations are a simply wonderful way of protection and shelter.

Affirmations during midday or before lunch:
May all living beings be equally happy and in balance.
May all beings be safe and protected, happy and content.
I let go of all distress and fear, knowing to be safe.
This space is a sacred space of transformation.
In gratitude I bow to the higher personality within.

During the day, the higher personality is guiding us, and if one is attentive and listens, then grace and blessings come with inquiry.

As we ask, so we receive.
Here, honesty is most valuable.

Please, may I have shelter from lower conditions and stressful circumstances.

May I receive the shelter of your grace and be protected by calamities.

May all beings be kind and friendly.

May I serve for the highest of human.

Is there a higher truth?
I am just to see. Where shall I look?
What is the purpose of my life or this sitauation?

Some might call it the fourth and fifth dimension within the living entity. However, affirmations work through polarity and attraction. It is like a play of call and response. When having a sacred sound vibration or Mantra, like the Maha-Mantra Hare Krsna Hare Krsna Krsna Krsna Hare Hare Hare Rama Hare Rama Rama Rama Hare Hare then this can be sung in a certain way. Usually this affirmation in musical form is called kirtan or chanting of the holy name. There is a slight mystery and wonder within this process, therefore it is recommend to experience it.

When one is calling Hare Hare! Or Divine Light! Then, within the pause, there is an echo or answer. Something within reciprocates and gives resolution to what has been said or called out for.

Therefore, listening is so important. Listen to your inner voice and be aware of slight changes. Breathe in-between and notice differences and alterations.

<u>Affirmations to increase life satisfaction</u>

This meditation takes the form of a mantra. You can repeat the affirmations silently inside your mind or out loud if you prefer. Allow yourself to really feel the words and let them resonate.

Repeat each fresh phrase like a Kirtan, call and response.

I am satisfied with all there is,
Nothing more, nothing less,
Balance in equanimity,
Feel Peace and Harmony.
I am satisfied with you,
Content and true,
Here and Now,
I take a bow
Silence in my mind,
Love in my heart,
We are all a part
Of a wonder world,
From the breath,
From east to the west,
I Live to try the best.
I affirm to be content
Here and Now,
With All there is
On the way to bliss,
I bow, Balance is now
Silence in my mind,

Love in my heart,
We are all a part,
Of this moment world,
A Moment to Moment,
Breathe and feel,
Peace, Love and Unity
I affirm Harmony
Within all there is,
I am bliss,
I am Balance,
I am equanimity,
Peace, love and unity.
I meditate upon the Wholeness,
Balance for everyone,
Peace for everyone,
Love for everyone,
Unity for everyone,
Harmony for everyone,
Bliss for everyone
I meditate upon the Highest Absolute,
May you be merciful with Us,
May we serve for the highest good of all,
May we All live in Peace and Harmony.
Love and Unity,
Here and Now,
I bow.

Guided Breathing For: Relaxation

Creating space to relax - Create space for relaxation with the meditation. Become aware of your thought processes and any tendencies that accompany your experience of relaxation.
Start meditating. Focus on your breath, equally flowing in and out. Equally in, equally out. Bring your attention to the sound of the breathing. Calming, soothing breath, flowing in and out. Let it flow naturally and listen in. By listening we open our gates to the soul. The connection of sound and space lets us relax. Creating space, listening, relax with every breath.
Let the breath come and go. See yourself easing into the simple process of breathing. Nothing more, nothing less. Just the breath. Just feel. Relax. Every thought arising, every thought passing. Remember the breath, coming and going, and again equally in and out. The thoughts may come and go - no need to do anything - just breathe.

Now, when you notice a thought coming, observe it. Just see it as it is and let it be. Like the breath, here to make us live. Feel the life with every breath. Feel the sensation of the chest rising with every inhale. Once you feel, just be aware of the sensation of the area around the heart. If you cannot feel, slightly hard breathe. Just a few times intensely breathing in, making space, being aware of the free flow. Let it flow naturally. According to the breathing thoughts may come and go. Just observe and be aware of any thought springing up. Let it flow, let it go, let it be. Feel free. With every breath, equally in, equally out. Sometimes the stream of thought is very strong, carrying us away, be attentive and aware. With a balanced mind we come home to our breathing. Naturally to the present moment with the power of the breath. Maintain balance and equanimity. Let the stream of thoughts just evenly be, relax and feel free. Feel free. Equanimity. Relax.

<u>A vision of relaxation</u>

Create a vision of relaxation in your mind. By focusing in on that mind picture, you can deepen your physical and mental experience of relaxation.
The thought, the breath, live with us. Relax and trust yourself, we are aware, we are alive. Like on a mindful journey on the beach, sandy feet, our thoughts come to the shore like waves, carried by the wind. Every wave a thought, just coming to shore and sinking into the ground. Observe and be aware of your breath. Listen. The in and out, equally in, equally out.

Breathe naturally and hear the sounds of the waves. No need to do anything, just be present and aware. Balance your breath and let yourself be safe at shore, trust. Your whole body comes to ease, to peace, to just relax. Observe the vast space of the ocean, the horizon, the endless tide. Coming and going, see the wind carry the waves to shore. Be aware of the nature of the breath. Now maintain this image until even this one is flowing away. A space of peace and balance, every thought we trust, we accept and let be. May there be any sensation, prickling, tingling, vibrating, warm or cold, lightness, numbness, any sensation, any thought, any wave, just observe and see it coming and going, like the breath. Pain, sorrow, hardship, just a thought, as it comes and goes, so impermanent, so it comes to shore, and we smile. Smile in gratitude, in peace, in joy. Ease in. Relax.
Evenly breathe and deepen your breathing. Inhale. Exhale, and see the body be just a body, see the mind just as it is. Observe the depths of the breath. Rising and passing away. Rising and passing away. Ease in. Relax.

<u>Becoming aware of relaxation</u>

This is a meditation where you will rest in awareness. By doing so you can consciously start to become more aware of the sensations that accompany relaxation.

Find the ease, be aware of the breathing naturally flowing, be aware of every sensation of the body. Wherever a sensation arises be sure it passes eventually. Whatever it is; Tingling, Prickling, Vibrating, Warmth, Cold, lightness, numbness, whatever it may be, be sure it passes eventually. Just observe and see that you don't label it, be aware that whatever and wherever it happens, it is just happening in the moment. May All sensations be equally observed. Equally with a balanced mind.

A mind that is resting on awareness, a still mind that is actively attentive, a mind that knows all the patterns. Rising and passing away, a constant coming and going, impermanent, ever changing. The nature of the sensations is there to transform. Just relax and observe the changes, the rising and passing away, the nature of impermanence. Keep yourself calm, keep a still and balanced mind. Equal at any time.

Breathe evenly, in and out. Evenly observe any sensation with a balanced mind. With a calm and equanimous mind. Still there might be sensations that make us feel in a way and it is all ok, just go with the feeling for awhile, befriend it, trust it, be even and do not judge or label it. As it is a part of your life it surely has its place. Give it space, let it rest, let it be and feel free. An endless lake of awareness, so still, so calm, so beautiful. Any ripple is to be observed, and when the mind is so quiet, than we may have a glance to the bottom of the lake.

There we may see our life, just as it is. See it with an equanimous mind, always aware and attentive. Balanced and calm mind. In the stillness we can see. In the beauty we feel free. Every sensation, every thought, let it be, relax and breathe.
Cultivating relaxation - This meditation has specifically been designed to assist you to cultivate relaxation. Purposefully practising relaxing makes it an easy state to enter at will.

Whenever you feel agitated, out of balance and Harmony, see the truth as it is. Every moment is ever-changing and impermanent. Every sensation is ever in transformation. Every thought comes and goes,
nothing is here to stay, except our divine peace and happiness. Practice this divine peace and happiness and all the imbalance will fade, pass away to change into absolute equanimity. By the practice with focus on the object of the breath, we attentively watch our friend. Our breath is accompanying us every moment of our life and therefore we come back to the breath. To be present. To be alive. We keep our focus with the breathing to stay present and harmonious, with breath, there comes Life.

There is life within awareness. Is the breathing calm and equal, the awareness can travel peacefully with our life. Is the flow of breath in peace, our life likewise is. Therefore focus on the breathing, patiently and persistently, observing, seeing the everlasting changes and be aware of all the sensations. Whatever arises will come and go, rise and pass away. Focus on the small area from the upper lip to the nostrils and watch the breath moving in, and moving out again. Intensely inhale once and maintain the focus on that part of the face, with absolute awareness of the breath. Maintain and cultivate awareness of the breath, befriend it and let it be the friend for life, evenly flowing, naturally growing our sense of Self. Trust that there is Harmony and Peace, know that the breath is there. Relax and breathe.

In a Single moment of uncertainty, find truth in the reality of life. Breathing is real and essential. Breathe and evenly, patiently give yourself the trust to be your own master. Practice diligently and cultivate mastery over the breathing. In and out, equally, evenly, in balance and Harmony, we can be. Practice patiently and persistently. Breathe equanimously. Relax.
Reflecting upon relaxation - What does it mean to relax? Where do you go to the relax? What do you do to relax? Sit in reflection in this meditation session and contemplate the meaning of relaxation.

Sit with an equanimous mind. Start again the practice and remind yourself. Remind your senses of the peace and harmony of relaxation. Remember all the moments of joy that make you feel in balance. Imbalance comes from habit, so think and focus on habits that make you feel relaxed... make up an image of yourself, smiling and at peace. Where this place is, only you personally know, only one Self knows truly. See yourself sitting, smiling, simplifying. To see yourself in relaxation, to observe a thought and to know it's truth. Do you spend time with your friend, the breath, the everlasting bond to life, or do you do something else? Do you go to the beach, the Forrest or to the mountains to see yourself happy, at peace, in relaxation?

Whatever you do, practice makes it happen, so what you practice every day makes your life. So? Think of the best moments of joy and happiness, be aware of the great joys in life. Smile and remember the upbeat, heartfelt moments of bliss. Smile and dissolve into the divine peace & harmony. Breathe and feel alive. Relax. Give thanks, give appreciation and gratitude to your Self. Your breath, your thoughts, your sensations all are here for your life. Reflect your life in the stillness of awareness.

Allow yourself to dwell in peace, in mind and thought. Contemplate on the true essence of relaxation. Practice, master and cultivate all you need for a life of yours. With the power of the breath and the equanimity of mind, we connect to all living beings, to all the universe, to the truth within our Self. Be true to yourself, relax and trust the breath. Breathe and smile gently, feel the balance within body, mind and Soul. Come once more back to the sound of breathing and listen in. Be aware. Meditate. Relax.

<u>The upwards journey along the spine</u>

We journey into our body to discover the vast possibility of our spine, the Axis of the Universe. Together we traverse many lands to find a heavenly gate.
We imagine our spine as a ladder to heaven. The spine is an endless possibility to travel with awareness along this mystical path to freedom.
Everyone finds a comfortable seat. As we feel the Ground our body becomes naturally adjusted to the earth. As we sit we make sure our buttocks is equally balanced on both sides. Left and right, yang and yin are in harmony. We come to ease closing our eyes and imagining our being safely surrounded by a bubble of shimmering golden light. (Sound from singing bowl, gong)

See the bubble around you and be aware that this bubble protects, nurtures and allows you to travel everywhere in in your mind. So as we are all set, we prepare to visit one of the most important places of our human body, some call it the Axis of the Universe, it is that important - the spine.
First feel the spine as you sit and breathe.

We inhale, gently breathe and let the air travel to the ground you are sitting on. Visualize the very Fundament of your being, the core, the ground. Here, everything is still, like an infinite sea of energy. We travel with our golden light bubble to this land and sit on the lake, so beautiful and pristine. See the lake, does it sit still and quiet, or does it ripple waves? Observe and be aware, the stillness is essential.
So we can witness the life air.
Breathe in and out.
Streaming in, the air flows downwards, breathing out we see the motion upwards.
Repeat this breathing for a while and watch the lake, what is happening to it?
Breathe in, let the air settle in, breathe out, let it rise.
While we find ourselves safe in the Golden Light Bubble, we witness the reflection of the sun, right on this lake. The beautiful glitter, sparkling and endlessly moving.
The lake is like a mirror for the sky, the beautiful shining of heavens light up above.

While we look into the horizon We see a mystical bird using the upwards air to hover in a vortex to the sky. The graceful beauty and stunning ease of the birds wings make us free and we join the bird. We get closer and closer to the wind vortex, and slowly step into the air moving up. Light like a bird we move up. Like God has given us wings we hover with the warm air to a new height. Slowly ascending, we lift to the peaks of mountains, looking

over the land. Look and see the trees, green and lush, see the lake peacefully floating, be aware of the suns light. Our golden bubble protects us and keeps us safe. Even in midst the body, vertebrae by vertebrae, breath by breath we gently come into harmony and alignment.
Coming closer to the Sky.
Our wings are getting stronger, our breath is heavier. Breathe intense. Let it out through the mouth and continue on. Relax the jaw, feel free to lay down, make yourself comfortable as we are slowly approaching a magnificent golden gate with a guardian, strong and fierce he greets us.

It is the Heartkeeper who knows us, smiles and welcomes us in devotion. We put our hands together, bow and greet him with a smile. We stop close to Him and observe His form. Like a hero, a legendary warrior for peace, he says: Follow the Air and the Sun, now your journey has only begun. Enter and find the Palast of your heart, this one is all a kingdom longing to serve the good.
Smile, be happy and enjoy.
The Heartkeeper bows again and opens this huge golden gate, we enter in, within.

Lift up your chin, let the focus be on the nose tip, and breathe. This is the Garden of Heaven, a Kingdom for Good, a Palast for You. Everything in here is true and meant to be for you.
Give yourself a moment to hold this image and repeat:
I am safe and sound I am safe and sound I am safe and sound
You be safe and sound You be safe and sound You be safe and sound
We are safe and sound We are safe and sound We are safe and sound
Relax and take a seat on your throne, a golden throne overlooking all the land. Rely on the golden light that protects, and send it back all the way. Let the golden light sink into the smallest, even tiniest part of the world. Every little piece shall be fulfilled. So the golden light shines throughout the world and illuminates every house, every village, every city and everyone's home.
(Have a candle or light inside)
Now you can imagine everyone happy and fulfilled with the light from your throne. Now you can visualize a little smile on everyone's face as you see the Heartkeepers smile.

Now let the whole Axis of the Universe shine with golden light and see the stars, the galaxies and cosmic entities be nurtured with this light. As we now see all the universes illuminated, we can now illuminate this room.
(Play soothing music preferably gong, singing bowl)
Slowly and gently we come to our private universe, gently we come with awareness to our bodies, smoothly we breathe and let the life air fulfill us with love and light.

Rub your palms to create warmth on each side, rub and put them on your face. Let them be like a warming bath in bliss. Smile and enjoy. The hands can now spread this bliss all over the body, all over, especially there where it is needed.
Feel free to sigh of relief.
HAAA, HUUU, HMMM
Come to the here and now.
Fold your hands and bow.
Make a sound like wooow.
Open your eyes, give thanks, Namaste

Self-Love

<u>Cultivating Joy</u>

Here we nurture the soil of long-lasting inner happiness, satisfaction and joy.
From within to All.
Joy, Happiness, Peace

Be aware of your natural flow of respiration. The natural breath. Life. Coming in and going out. Whatever comes, it goes. Even love and joy, come and go. Breathe all the joy, let it flow out into the world. See all the beings within a golden light of joy. Let this golden stream be and find the joy inside. What is making me joyful now? What brings me lasting joy? Finding the core, finding the peace and harmony. First we still the mind by breathing. Joy, with the matter of happiness and lightness coming from that source. Stillness. Awareness. Happiness. Breathing in, stillness comes, breathing out, restlessness goes. Ease in and naturally breathe. Let it flow. Let all the joy come and let it go. Thoughts may come, thoughts may go. Keep a balanced mind and find joy within this equanimity. Find peace and harmony from the ease of the breathing. Life is there. Breath opens the gates to joy. See it open and observe the joy as it is. Observe and be aware of the natural flow. Feel it sinking in, into the heart, into the root. Now breathe deeply into the root, into the ground, to cultivate to nature the soil of joy. Breathe with all the attention and love. See your breathing moving to the root, feel the bottom of the belly and be aware of the heart. Silence yourself. Keep stillness for a moment and come out again with your unique voice. Chant and repeat.

I am the Joy of the World
I am the joy of the world
I am I am I am the joy of the world

You are the joy of the world
You are the joy of the world
You are, you are, you are the joy of the world

We are the joy of the world
We are the joy of the world
We are, we are, we are, the joy of the world.

Blissfully we can hold a kingdom of peace and harmony. With the matter of the breath we are alive. How wonderful life is. Breathing in and out, a constant flow of joyful air comes by to celebrate with us. To celebrate life. To conquer misery. Breathing in and breathing out. Finding balance within and knowing the inner source of joy. Flowing through every vein, into every part of the body, from head to feet we observe a continuous flow of joyful bliss within. Equally flowing along the spine into all the energy centres.
Equally, including all the layers of our being, from most subtle to gross, joy permeates all our being with wonderful light. It reaches our skin and touches our heart. It comes to the nostrils and flows in and out. Balance yourself, enjoy the flow, rest and relax.
Namaste

Cultivating Compassion

Sit in a comfortable position, relax, your spine and shoulders are in balance. Your head is slightly turned upwards, loosening the head from the throat and chest area with a slight shake. Open your hands palms facing upwards, let the position be steady and grounded.
We are now growing until we are a Giant that can hold the whole world within Ones hands. We are growing physically, mentally and will grow our compassion for the whole wide world, every insect, every plant, animal, human All included.

You are now well grounded sitting on your buttocks and relaxing into the breath. The Life streams into the nostrils and unfolds as Great Compassion. In a wonderful golden stream, an endless string of air flows in, and back out. Be aware of the Great Compassion spreading in your being. With every breathing in we grow. Our chest raises, the belly comes out. Within the belly we feel the expansion of our feelings of compassion. Our belly lights up in a serene golden light. We grow with every breath. With every exhalation we free ourselves, expanding more and more. Now we close the eyes gently and see ourselves growing and expanding, every part of our being expands and grows endlessly. We feel the heart, we are aware of the breath. Now we even grow out of our

room, we grow larger then the land, we are expanding as far as the universe. See the Earth being a little blue ball, we can easily hold in our hands. Being compassionate means to be all-inclusive. We see and accept all the life that is on this vast and beautiful planet. We can see all living beings on this earth together. We can see our homes and the homes of others. We are aware of all the life, on this one planet. We hold this precious blue ball in our hands, we are bringing the hands together and feel compassionate. We are bringing our hands with our planet to our hearts. All-accepting we give a slight bow and a gently smile to the whole world.

I am compassion You are Compassion We are Compassion For all living beings
I am compassion You are Compassion We are Compassion For all living beings
I am compassion You are Compassion We are Compassion For all living beings
Feel the Compassion sink in, and let the earth be. Allow yourself to grow back to normal size and see the whole world become our ground again. Feel the Ground of the earth and be aware of your breathing. Loose your head, neck and shoulders. Bring your palms together and chant: Om Shanti, Shanti, Shanti

The old Me

Imagine yourself in your older Self asking questions, receiving answers, inner guidance, inner eternity.
Find a comfortable position and start to be aware of the breath. From the nose tip to the entrance of the nostrils notice the sensation of the life air moving in. Into the body, let the air flow in and out again. Be aware of all the sensations while the air enters the nostrils. Is it more on the right, or more on the left side of the nose.
Is the breathing equal? Slow and subtle or harsh and intense? Find comfort in the process of breathing. Find a comfortable seat and your root grounded to the soil. Your spine is erect. See your spine and neck align having your whole body in balance and comfortable.

Close your eyes. Take a deep intentional inhale, and let go. Whatever thought arises, keep breathing, in and out. Breathe naturally. Come to ease and visualize your self sitting here, just breathing. See yourself in a light of peace and comfort. See yourself with a smile. Now imagine, your body is aging, with every breath, every moment. It is not so bad, your spirit keeps young at heart, eternally. It is just your body and soon enough it will be as wrinkly and used as your life goes on. Life goes on, with experience, you become wise and grow wiser and wiser. Just in your mind, just with the imagination. The breath comes and goes and now see yourself very old and very wise, with deep marks of experiences on your skin and a gentle smile. You have become old! And wise. To be wise means you know all you know from experience. So you have been through many experiences and can now answer any

question. Any question about life. Listen and see your old self respond, wait and take your time. Concentrate on the heart and feel, it is just the body. Just the age taking over the body, just imagine and smile.
You can ask, what will keep me young, what will make me happy?
And the wise old self responds, naturally taking time. Respect the age of the body, know the mind and see your self with every single breath becoming younger and younger, the skin becomes very soft, the breathing lighter and lighter. You become even as little and innocent as a little baby. See yourself as beautiful as pure, just observe your inner innocence, your inner Child. Slowly and gently smile and knowing it is just the body, the mind keeps in balance. See your self in all the forms you like... the body may change but we always keep young at heart, always in spirit eternal. As you come back to the nose and the air flowing in, you come back the present body. Thankful as we are, we give thanks and appreciation to the present state of being. Gratitude to all the experience that make us who we are and Compassion to all beings likewise, as we all age, our body may differ but we all age. It is a natural, simple process, like we know our family, we all are on the same path. Giving a smile to our loved ones, giving gratitude and compassion to all alike. May all beings be happy and safe. Breathe and relax into the prayer. Pray for Peace, Harmony and balance. Bring the hands together and bow in serenity, namaste.

Rainbow Garden

Experience the full spectrum of colors and forms by visualization nature and observe how it makes you feel

Sit in a comfortable position and relax into the breath. Bring your awareness to the nostrils where the air enters the nose. Be aware of the breathing and equally inhale and exhale. Balance your body on the ground and listen to the sound of nature. (Playing singing bowl, flute, gong) Give yourself time and space to enter a beautiful garden full of colours and possibilities. See the wonderful earth of the garden, a nice brown-red tone unfolds and we see the texture of the soil... feel the earth and smile, this garden is to grow your favourite plants. So we imagine we have a handful of seeds, open your palms facing upwards and now gesture like you are spreading the seeds on this earth. The seeds are wonder seeds and plants now grow in all colours in all shapes and forms. We see our favourite sorts of oranges, just growing from the seed to tree to fruit, we see wonderful flowers shining in bright yellows and golden, we see the leaves of many many plants in everlasting green. So around us there unfolds a field of wonderful colours all growing up to the nice blue sky.

Of course all these plants need good nurturing of water, so we ask kindly if the rain wants to gives us fall. We look up to the sky and the clouds are coming in, spreading around and the sky gets darker and darker, the clouds move in and let big magic rain drops fall onto the earth. The water is nice and warm, we open up our hands and receive the rain. Feel how you are growing and growing. See how the plants are

growing and growing. (Rainmaker sounds)
Enough of the rain and the light of the sun comes pushing the clouds away. The brightness of the light reflects on the last rain drops and breaks down into a wonderful rainbow, shining in its most beautiful serenity. Visualize and hold this image of the purple, blue, sky blue, green, yellow, orange, red bowing down to your garden. Bring your palms together and bow down as well. Say Namaste and invite all your friends to your garden. Come gently back into the room and take all your time to remember these magic seeds from where all the colours came.
Focus your attention to the middle of the eyebrows and make a face. Create the tension and Hold the tension, hold, hold, and release. Your hands can now join to let the the face bathe in beautiful loving and healing energy. Bring your palms together and
Give yourself a big thanks. You have the rainbow within you, whenever you like to see the rainbow just ask the rain to come.
Rest and relax.
Namaste

Oneness Breath

Be One with yourself, with the world and the breath. Everything is connected. All beings may be surrounded in joy.
Joy, Oneness, Breath.
We start our journey on our magic mat, we sit firmly and grounded. We feel our bottom on the floor and erect the spine. The head is in one line with the main channel, the spine, neck and lower back. As we see ourselves in a safe and secure space, we start to close our eyes gently and softly, half closed, half opened. Breathing naturally, breathing normal. With every breath we become lighter and lighter, softer and finer the breath goes. Comes back in and flows back out. The more balanced we breathe the better we can now float. Every cell in the body becomes light and is filled with a wonderful glowing light of peace and joy.
We become lighter and lighter, lifting with our magic mat to new heights.
We lift higher and higher to the higher peaks of the world to have a good view on all that is happening. We have a panoramic view of the wide wonderful world.
Start to observe. The whole world in your breath. All the life that breathes is alive. Even the small pieces and parcels, even the plants and trees, even the bees and butterflies, even the animals, humans, all beings alike. All breathing, all alive. Just breathe, be with joy, breathe out. Let it flow. See yourself in a joyful glow of shining golden light. With every breathing expanding. Expand your light from the inside out, from

the core to the universe. Breathe. Joy travels with the breath, so see all the beings with this golden light of joy, even in the smallest particle, see the light boundlessly expanding into the world, into the universe. Meet the sun, joyfully shining the light onto the world. See all the world connected to that light and observe yourself in this joyful light. Breathe into this light and be aware of every sensation. Be aware of the natural flow of the breathing. In and out. Every breath connects us to the world, to every being. All the joy is with us, glowing in a beautiful golden light. See the sun, see the joy, observe yourself and be aware of the balanced breath. In and out, observe, equally in and out. See your family, watch them happily be. Set yourself free and smile. With all the joy, all the happiness. May all the joy and happiness surround me.
Breathe. Enjoy.
May all the Joy surround me.
Palms together, in front of the chest, let the thumbs touch the heart. May all the joy surround me.
Bow.
May All the Joy surround me,
Namaste.

Insomnia

Purity

This purity shall help us to be aware of past attractions, therefore the meditations are dedicated to clean the mirror of the heart-mind, which is full of material dust.

Through conscious breathing, the mirror can be cleansed and one can see the truth within. Natural desires and thoughts are arising and passing, equally as the breathing arises and passes.

Everything, like ebb and flood, comes and goes, but what we have attracted is still present with us. Therefore, we use a special technique of meditation to reduce the mind-clutter and to make space for pure attraction.

Pure attraction comes in form of a person to you. The Person is the Highest Person, and Absolute Truth. Situated in the temple of the heart lingering on the lake of consciousness. This Absolute Truth is sitting on a nice patio, with a beautiful seat made of the softest cushion grass. The Supreme Person is clothed in silk and finest wool, decorated with abundant jewels, amulets, golden bangles and a beautiful flower garland.

This highest Supreme Person is the source of all abundance and attraction. The name of this person is Krishna, which means the all-attractive one. All-attractive. So whatever you can imagine, whatever you have ever dreamed of, whatever is possible and impossible is granted through the permission of this Highest Person.

The Supreme Personality sits within the heart of every living being, and one can address this spiritual state as follows:

'O, Supreme Attractor, please grant me access to the realm of consciousness where all is possible. I am hungry for attraction and abundance. Please allow me a bite of this transcendental joy and bliss. May all beings be happy.'

Contemplate, and breathe. Sit comfortably and stay in this consciousness for a moment. Become aware of the stillness of the lake, and just notice the mind focusing its intention on the longing for attraction.

Breathe, and just accept this moment as it is, the Supreme Personality is hearing and listening.

For a moment, come to ease and listen to the matter of the breathing, how it is still present, knowing to be alive.

Give thanks and gratitude to the present moment, in mind, word and action. Fold your palms together, in front of the chest and be aware of the subtle energetic currents flowing from the palms and along the arms, shoulders, neck, head and heart.

A natural hunger or lusty desire is attracting whatever one is open to receive. However, before we can accept any outer circumstance, one has to accept the inner circumstance. Therefore, by approaching the Supreme reservoir of all attraction one has direct access to unlimited resources within. This resource comes in form of conscious waves of energy.

Prepare and be aware, whatever you like to attract is just a connection. Not so far away, but the more precious and kindly we ask, the better one can receive.

Open the hands and palms facing upwards. This gesture helps to let go of unwanted and unnecessary clutter in mind and energy. Just surrender and let your palms face to the sky. Breathe equally, and relax. Everything is fine, we are just about to clean the mirror of the heart and mind with simple sounds.

Pure Sunshine Meditation

Just sit, together with the Supreme Person who is very beautiful and renounced on the lake of consciousness. It is almost sunrise, and the sky is glowing very beautifully. See the stars and planets on the firmament, these are like all the persons, forefathers, masters, saints and heavenly beings in innumerable numbers. Knowing the sun comes up, the Supreme reservoir of light unfolds.
The rays of this sunlight spread internally and externally, from within the solar-plexus translucent light is emanating around the heart, shoulders, arms, hands, hips, legs, feet and head. The bliss and energy of the sunshine spreads around the whole being and warmth is present.

The horizon now gives a sense of smile. Golden and brilliant, the effulgence of the sun purifies all the senses and equips one with happiness and comfort.

Consciously breathe and equally feel the breath. Rhythmically in and out again. Very equal, and with an equanimous mind. The light of the sunshine makes one smile, and happiness and joy are attracted, like flowers of a tree blossom when touching the sunlight.
Smile, be happy and content. All the joy, happiness and love is surrounding you.

Offering and Receiving pure Love

If it would be sold in a shop everyone would buy it. Love. It comes from the heart and is the essential force that connects us humans, person to person. Its divine quality is bliss and truthfulness.

So, just sit under that desire tree and imagine yourself to be very nicely situated in a peaceful. mode of observance. Seeing the cows grazing on the field, listening to the birds in the sky and being aware of the subtle sensation of the life air streaming into the nostrils and out again.
Equally, breathe, and feel the touch of the roots. The lower back, buttocks or whole body may be equally touching the ground. Envision an energetic connection with the ground and also with the heart. From the heart, light illuminates the sight and one can see the spring in the garden of one's heart. The tree is giving a nice shelter before the morning sunshine.

By breathing one can consciously access this garden of hearts, where even friends and family can take a rest. Just call out to someone and see the connection to this person. A loved one might be just waiting to be invited. Love is all you need, just connect to your loved one and let the force act. Love is intelligent, natural life force. Just be a channel for this energy and submit. Smile and be happy, because your loved one is just appearing at the entrance of the garden.

Wonderful as it seems, but your friends have no shoes on! Where there is a beautiful lush garden with soft grass, ain't no one needs shoes. Greetings and a warm welcome, there is enough space under the tree. Just feel free and breathe.

It's okay to dream away, however one may be aware of the breath. Whenever there is doubt, fall, or fear, just breathe. Breathing brings balance. 'Here you are invited to wish for a nice fruit', says the desire-tree. Just speak or think it out, what would you like. The desire-tree is providing you and your friend. Cheesecake? No problem, the desire-tree is a wish-fulfilling desire-tree and no desire remains open. It can read your mind.

Speaking of the mind. The mind is like a well that can provide the necessary contact for abundance. If you have a full mind-well, well, that's good, because then one can fetch from the mind-well and give away the awareness. Awareness is the potency from a mindful reservoir. When the mind is empty, well, then it is easy to fill up. Is the mind full, well then, one can fetch awareness from this well. Awareness of attention is the attraction towards the sense objects. While. meditating, one can notice these sense objects and senses to attach, and detach. Once there comes a subtle stream of air, it touches the skin, one can feel, but then it fades just like the breeze fades. Same with sound, taste, smell and sight. Of all the senses and sense objects form, shape and colour are the most attractive, especially to the eyes.

This is why one can envision a garden of wonderful trees or one can determinedly stare at the nose-tip. Both has an effect and keeps the mind busy and attached. To detach the mind, one can use the hands, clapping once or twice. This sound is very powerful and overpowers the attached senses easily.

Just consciously attach your mind and focus towards an object of desire, maybe an apple or a banana, or a cheesecake. Put all the energy of attention into the process and remain still, for a moment, let go. Smile, and offer the desired object to your dear friend or loved one. Leave the breathing natural and see.
Mindfulness can be a process of loving transmission. One can even give love to others just by thought. Further, when the mind is engaged in loving transmission connecting to a higher wish or desire, the senses become fixed. Focusing the mind on the nice form of the Supreme Personality, the origin of all abundance, the. All the senses are automatically engaged in the service of the mind. Then, smelling can be very inspiring, hearing a wonderful experience, seeing a miraculous occasion, touching a blissful act, and tasting a joyful endeavour.
Mindfulness can lead to abundance by steady application and determination, as well as faith.

In meditation, one can access these realms of subtle energies, like the lake of consciousness.
Here, many seeds of desire are stored, and these seeds again act as potential outcomes.

<u>Offer a Smile</u>

Just sit mindfully with your loved one under that tree within the garden of your heart and breathe. Consciously, rhythmically and equal. Find a smile and also offer this to your friend. Love attracts, and the more attention we give, the more on can reciprocate. Just see your friend from the bottom of the sole, to the tippy toes, along the ankles, calves, knees, thighs, and the upper body. How is this loved one dressed, and what special features can you make out? See the upper body and chest, the arms, hands and fingers. Finally, see the neck, chin, jaw and eyes. See the eyes and forehead. Smile gently, and see your loved one as a meditative companion who has always been within the garden of your heart.

This is even how to attract associates, ad loving relationships. We can desire nice friendships and good relations, and of course one can meditate upon these. One who has a spiritual teacher knows, it is best to see from the feet to the head.

Give thanks and appreciate the community. Be aware of this eternal moment within the garden of the heart, underneath that desire tree. Watch the lake of consciousness be very nice and still. The sunshine of the midday is reflecting within the waters stillness and here swans and cranes are playing in the rear.

Beyond the beautiful lake of consciousness, there are mountains of steadiness and determination, and even upon the peaks, one can see a little reflection of the sunshine. Within the trees, there are plenty of flower blossoms and fruits. Many beautiful leaves are dancing within the wind and the sound of birds is most enchanting. The subtle breeze charms with a sweet aroma of forest fruits.

You and your friend are in meditative harmony, just breathing and enjoying. There is nothing to do, there is no must, no stress, just endless happiness. Blissfully dreams come true, and a slight bluish hue reflects from the lake of consciousness.

A meditative dream bird lands nearby within a forest grove. It is a very colourful bird, with black, purple, silver and blue feathers. Can you guess what kind of bird is this?

<u>Attracting Peace of Mind:</u>

Find a comfortable seat. Breathe equally in and out, find your ground and balance as you erect your spine. Gently look upwards, open the throat area and relax the shoulders.
Bring both palms together and chant a Mantra for Peace:
Om Shanti Shanti Shanti x3
Close your eyes, open your hands upwards, create a smile and find yourself watching the life air. See the breath moving into the nostrils and out again. See yourself sitting in a nice and lush forest close to a spring. A wonderful soothing sound sparkles next to you and calms your mind. (Play watery sounds) Listen and find ease.
While we sit in this forest we can hear the sounds of birds (play sounds of birds) and there comes a beautiful peacock, gracefully stepping out of the forest.
A shimmering blue feather cloak opens and we see the full splendid form. We hold the image, all feathers spread widely shining in silver, purple and white. The top of the crown-like wings hosts a beautiful eye. Innumerable eyes are wide-spread around the peacock, who greets us:
'Hello, peace be with you. Welcome to our blissful paradise. I am Padala.'
We smile. Smile and give thanks to the moment and Padala, the Peacock.
Padala says, 'come and explore the wide land on my back.'
We hop on and start our journey. Breathe and feel the lightness come with every breathing, in and out. With every breath we feel lighter and lighter, lifting up the sky above. 10 meters off the ground, 20 meters of the ground, 40 meters of the ground. We lift higher and higher with every breath we take. 100 meters of the ground, we can see the crowns of the trees, the peaks of the mountains and in the far, the endless horizon.
We fly in one direction and fly intensely. Breathe and breathe intensely. We are safe with Padala, so start to watch your breath again equally going in and out.
'I will bring you to my master, he lives in the paradise valley.'
We come to fly and see there is a vast green valley with a sacred stream and many abundant flowers and fruits. We come closer and closer, 100 meters, 80 meters, 40 meters, we breathe through and slowly get

a feel of this paradise valley. A Lush and plentiful scent of the land makes us feel peaceful. 20, 10, 1 meter off the ground, we slowly descent with Padala down to the green valley field.

We sigh of relief and gasp for fresh air. The land smells nicely and we find the beautiful Padala walking us to a small little hut, where a shimmering light protects the entrance. Only you can come here with your companion and guide Padala. We open the door and in this little hut there sits a person, so familiar and wise, the face shines in a transcendental glow of joy and happiness. We recognize this face and observe a warm welcoming smile. We smile back and give thanks for the invite to the masters home.

'You have come a long way, take rest and come to ease. We will have tea soon.' The masters long white robe shimmers of purity and wisdom. We will hold the stillness and peace for a while so one can ask any question to the wise master.

(Holding silence)

We breathe and come out of the silence for another smile.

, Here', the master says, 'take this favourite feather and you will be welcome everywhere you go, just open it for the host to see.'

The master gives us a feather.

'This feather is a sign of peacefulness and lightness, keep it dear to your heart.'

We accept and bow in reverence.

We leave and come back to The Valley. We breathe and come back to our body, we sigh and come back to the room. Chant Om Shanti, Shanti, Shanti.

Frieden, Peace, Shalom.

Close your palms together, give thanks to the peacock Padala, the master and all living beings alike.

Happiness Meditation

Be aware of the breathing. Moment to Moment one can notice how the breathing is equally streaming in and out. The breath is very subtle yet profound, streaming into the nostrils and flowing to the heart. From here the whole life air is distributed all over the body. The body is charged with life energy and happiness.

Happiness can come in many ways, but the easiest is light. Light is always present and can be transformed into anything one likes to attract. The human body is like a magnet with two poles, and like light, it has a dual character. When there is balance in the body through meditation. Happiness can ignite a fire of freedom and bliss.

So, breathe equally and mindfully. The mind is sometimes compared to a flickering lamp, but one who is steady in meditation can easily still the flickering of the lamp. This is the purpose of meditation.

See this lamp, or candle within your vision and know that from one candle one can ignite many more candles, easily this can be done from a simple hand.

Sit equally and in a comfortable position. Put one hand on the area of the navel and breathe equally. Feel, how the belly rises and sinks with every breath. With inhalation, the belly rises, and with exhalation, the belly sinks to normal.

Just be aware of the balance between inhalation and exhalation. Let it be the basis for a steady and happy meditation.

An endless source of happiness is found within the heart, therefore, let's focus on the heart and its beat. This beat is the rhythm of one's life. Now, put one hand onto the chest and feel the heartbeat.

Be aware and notice its character, what does the heart say? What is within the heart's desire? Is the rhythm equal and in harmony?

Just notice the beats and sit straight. Now, use your hand to move in a clockwise circle around the chest area and belly. Let it be a flowing movement, connecting both heart and belly.

Breathe, and smile.

Now, use the hands to swipe the other parts of the body. Just swipe. Eventually, one can do this sweeping with the awareness, cleansing the whole body, energy and mind.

Now, come back to the heart and happiness. Smile, again. Breathe equally in and out. Let the smile sink into the heart and remember a moment of happiness within your life. Maybe just very recently, what did make you considerably happy?

Let it be a simple thing, like a smile, and continue seeing this memory to be present and within the heart. Let the memory pass, and breathe equally.

Be aware of your whole body. Now, remember a person that makes you especially happy. See this person in form and character, with full heart and within the inner vision. Be aware of the moment with the person, right here within the heart. Breathe and let it sink into the garden of the heart. Welcome to the lake of consciousness, where everybody is fully in balance, peace and happiness.

The Supreme Abundance greets also from this place of the heart. Breathe equally and come to ease. Sweet birds are flying around the sacred trees, making the atmosphere very wonderful and serene. Can you see the lake of consciousness? Is it still? Are you aware of the little sensations that are going on, maybe warmth or cold, tickling, throbbing, vibrating. Just focus on the heart and the garden of a happy heart.

All together with the Supreme Abundance who sits very comfortably on a cushioned throne overlooking the lake of consciousness, garlanded and scented very nicely, Supreme Abundance is smiling and inviting to have a comfortable position to see the sunset.

Happiness can be so simple, like watching a sunset together. The lake of consciousness is very nicely reflecting the effulgent rays of the sun, turning the whole atmosphere into a joyful place. As the golden globe enchants and enlights everything with a tranquil glow of happiness one can witness the sweet songs of the birds. A natural symphony creates balance within the system and here, in this heartful land, there is no lack of happiness.

One can be grateful and appreciative to be here, and now. Breathing equally in and out, in respect to nature and heaven. One can give thanks to the light, especially of the sun who provides blissful light to everyone.

By folding the hands together, and holding the palms on the chest, and in front of the heart one can speak the following affirmations:

Thanks Giving to the Light,
May all beings be happy,
Shine bright into the night,
May all beings be happy.

Even in the darkness,
There is happiness,
Love and Lightness,
always in bliss.

In every heart, and every breath.
In and out, equally breathe and relax.
Let the sunlight give healing and happy light to the core and notice that even the sunshine shines from within. A simple smile makes a perfect sun,
glowing and igniting the spark of happiness in everyone.

Now one can affirm happiness and prosperity in one's life:

May I attract happiness and love,
May all beings be happy and loved.
May love and happiness surround all.

Happiness shall fill my life,
My life and every life.
Happiness shall speak to me,
May all beings happy and free.

May prosperity be present,
May I see health and happiness.
Abundance for the world and I.
May all beings be happy and free.

Sit in a comfortable position and open the palms to the sky. Just receive. Be content and satisfied, happily awaiting the bliss.

It is already there, you see? Breathe and be happy.
Within endless energy of heart and soul, one can fetch the happiest of all: Life. From life comes love and from love comes life. Life is already filled with happiness, one just needs to be open, trusting and receptive.

Trust in your ability to trust and be patient, breath by breath a conscious relationship with the abundant heart takes place. This is the best way. Breathing equally, and remaining in balance. In and out, rhythmically, with great attention to the sensations. From the nose-tip to the heart, and from the heart to the belly. Happiness has taste and a wonderful feeling. Be aware of the emotional sensations and continue, giving attention to the heartbeat.

Envision a brilliant light pervading the matter of the body, flowing from the heart like a pure river of consciousness into the energy channels of the body. From the belly, the whole body is nurtured, likewise with energy. Therefore be aware of the light around the abdomen and let the awareness spread around the hips, legs, knees, ankles and feet. Let the light of awareness rise into the upper body parts again, streaming from the feet to the ankles, knees, thighs and lower body, to the upper body, chest, back, shoulders, arms and hands. Let the light of awareness now find the head. The neck, shoulders, jaw, chin and ears are all surrounded by beautiful, conscious light. Around the eyes, and on the crown of the head the light finds expression and blossoms into a sweet golden lotus flower.

See every petal of the lotus flower as a unique and magnificent creation. See it shining, embrace it and be aware that the lotus flower cannot be polluted, or contaminated. It has a protective layer that holds away all impurities. Embrace this pure golden lotus flower, and let it grow in the lake of consciousness.
Offer this lotus flower to the Supreme Abundance and hold the beauty and golden splendour of the sun within the heart. Breathe, equally in and out. Be aware of the sensations around the heart, body and mind.

Rest in this position and consciously focus on the nose-tip. By breathing in, one can connect a thought to the breath. By breathing out, one can let go of a thought. Be aware, and inhale with the thought of pure light. Exhale with the thought of letting go.
Inhale with the thought of golden happiness, exhale with the thought of letting go. Inhale with the thought of protection and peace, exhale and let go of fear, anxiety and pain.

With every breath, there is an exchange of energy and transformation happening. One can transform the subtle energy of the breath into life force, and thus attracting the life one desires. Through the permission of the Supreme Personality, one can receive all the protection, abundance and prosperity, health, happiness and freedom.

Depression & Positive Thinking

Reiki, please help us to release stagnating energy that needs to be relieved. Reiki, may I have your guidance and light to dissolve the unwanted energies. Let there be Reiki.
We tune into he Life Energy Reiki by opening our hands and asking for guidance. Simply ask.
Stress is mostly affecting our gut, inner organs, and nervous system, but can be relieved through the navel. Same with deep depression. It can be resolved as we come back to our mothers' life-giving channel. Place one hand for Reiki energy onto the navel, and another hand slightly higher from the chest, between the heart and throat chakra, to release and resolve the emotions that do not serve anymore. Imagine a wonderful healing flow streaming from the belly button to the heart center, from the heart to the throat, and slightly open your jaw, unclench and relax it. Let the energy flow for a good few minutes and wait so you feel the breathing. Breathing into the belly, breathing equally in and out, focus on the breath and feel the energy flow. Release the hands and give yourself a nice and soothing head and jaw massage. Release all tension and listen to soothing Reiki music.

Nurture and Compassion

Healing relationships and connections may be one of the higher goals in life. However, by healing ourselves, we heal others. By strengthening the connection to ourselves, our bodies, emotions and thoughts, we empower the connection to all around us. To nurture compassion and love put both of your hands onto the chest and you may be able to form a triangle with your fingers. Put this triangle on your chest and let it face in one direction. Feel and Embrace energy. Ask Reiki for Guidance and Help, Receive and Trust. Close your eyes and breathe naturally. A few minutes later, embrace change and alter the direction of the triangle to see the change. Breathe equally in and out. Relax and concentrate within the Heart space. Feel and energize your chest with a few deep breaths. Sink into meditation or play music.

<u>Beauty, Fame, and Communication</u>

Evenly Reiki can prosperously enhance our life quality by purifying our connection to ourselves and to our higher self. Energy can lead us on a journey to blissful realms of richness and abundance. The throat chakra resembles the sky and like the sky connects all beings, it is equally distributed for all. With one hand on the throat chakra and one below the navel, even the lower back we can harvest our inner beauty and receptivity for fame. Below the sky there is abundance, so is abundance within us. An infinite pool of energy. Let the Energy flow and ask Reiki kindly for help. 'Let there be Life force Energy.' Feel and breathe. Breathe into the belly and let the energy flow. Be aware of the breath and energy moving between throat and navel. Release the hands, lay down for a good relaxation and smile, smile gently.
Intuition and receptivity
Our Higher Self constantly transmitted messages to us, we just have to

listen in and tune into the radio of light. Reiki, please Guide Us with wisdom and light. Put one hand on the navel, to balance the body-mind and put one on the forehead on the third eye. Feel and breathe. While you are aware of any slight changes, smoothly move the lower hand from the navel to the heart. Feel again and be aware of any subtle sensation. Equally breathe in and out, close your eyes and imagine a beautiful bright light or a candle flame. May Reiki purify and guide us to wisdom and joy.
Release the hands, lay down for a good relaxation and maybe massage your temples or treat yourself with warm oil.
Be aware that all the chakras in the body are now balanced, only then it is advisable to balance the Crown Chakra.

Spiritual Growth

The crown on the top of your head connects us spiritually with the beyond, the endless, infinite space.
It is a bridge, like Reiki, to bridge the physical, emotional, mental and spiritual layers of our being. At the very end of spiritual growth, there stands absolute bliss, blossom like a graceful flower. Sit cross-legged and easy at your sacred spot and find the breathing to be equal and equanimous. Relax into the breath and ask Reiki for Guidance. Please, Reiki, Guide me.
Open the palms, hands on your thighs. Close your eyes and fully absorb the presence of Reiki. Feel free to let all thoughts lose and concentrate on nothing more than the sensation on the top of your head. One can imagine a beautiful blossoming flower that opens gently to the light of the sun. See all the beauty and grace unfold and give thanks to that moment, to Reiki and yourself.
Relax and Lay for rest.

Self-esteem. Shyness and Egoism

Feeling a stunning sense of self can sometimes be overwhelming or even a way to imbalance, however, it is all just the Solar energy stagnating or without a proper balance. Our hands help to focus and channel energy. Any kind of energy can be transmitted, but Reiki is the universal Life force which includes all energies. It heals and responds, intelligently finding the way.
Ask Reiki to heal, ask kindly to withdraw and receive energy from the source.
Breathe through, equally in and out, feel and receive Reiki energy. Be aware of the breath and focus on the entrance of the nostrils. Put your hand slightly below the chest and above the belly into the sternum. The solar plexus resides as nerves and knots within the body and takes care of the strength and power, acting as a channel between belly and brain. Put the other hand on the forehead or on the side of the head, close to the jaw and ear area. Energy shall flow between the brain, the third eye chakra, and solar plexus. Hold the position and breathe accordingly. Harmonize the breathing, equally in and out. Feel the energy rising, flowing along the spine. Any sensation may arise with it, warmth, tingling, vibrating, but one shall keep breathing naturally and normal. Remain and Relax, open the hands facing upwards to the sky and close the eyes for a few minutes. Feel and breathe.

Gratitude for Good

We make a journey to our inner most feeling of gratitude, for us and for all.
:
We find a comfortable seat and give our attention to Mother Earth and the Ground. Feel the buttocks, feel the whole body being steady and well nurtured. The roots, are spreading widely into the floor and one feels the main column, the spine in balance. Now let the body be an endless place of discovery. The breath is the vehicle for your journey. We are looking for a place of endless gratitude and thanks.
Gratitude for this world, for all the living beings, for your family and friends.
Imagine with every single breath you start to shrink, smaller and smaller, you become so small, you are fitting into the nostril, even smaller you are so small you can fit into an oxygen particle, a very tiny piece of existence. Now you travel with the wind breathing in and there you are inside your nose. Inside the body, flowing in an endless stream of air down the throat and chest area into the lungs. You start to feel light, so small and tiny. With every breath you become lighter and lighter, so light, you can fit into the space between the lungs. There is an open cave, mysterious and beautifully decorated, rose colored and shimmering with light, you can now see through the skin to the heart. Feel the lightness and meet the Heartkeeper, a wonderful friend and friendly warrior.

Protecting your Heart, he knows who you are and bows in a gracious manner. You can now enter, the Heartkeeper says and we enter. The wide Palast-alike spaces allow a beautiful freedom to dance, sing and what you like it to be. Now we fill this Palast with gratitude and you will see how this palace is so great it holds place for everyone you invite. Breathe naturally and let thanks flow in. Let the breathing be natural and let gratitude flow in. Breathe out and let it anger and sorrow go.

Hold your palms together and join a prayer: I am thankful for my family,
I am thankful for my friends,
I am thankful for all the beings. x3

We come gently back to our guardian the Heartkeeper and give thanks from All our Heart. There is a Heartkeeper in everyone of Us and we now see all connections. All our Hearts are connected. We see a World wide connection of Heartkeepers.

We hold stillness for a while. We let our breathing become natural and flowing. Gently we put our hands over our face. We feel and sense the warmth of the palms. We blink and gently open our eyes. We massage our face and come to ease. Give yourself all the time, and return back to your normal size into this room. Let the palms open on your laps and give thanks to every one in the room.

I am thankful for U
I am thankful for U
I am thankful for U

Breathing joy and satisfaction

We find satisfaction in the moment, not to do more, not to do less, just as it is, content, at peace and ease.

Acceptance, satisfaction, joy.
Find a comfortable seat. Breathe through. Like a big sigh, a relief, a liberation. A sigh of freedom. Imagine yourself on the peak of a mountain, totally liberated and free. Breathe the fresh air of fulfillment and be. Content you sit there and just breathe. See yourself just right there on the top, breathing and satisfied. Nothing to do, endless possibility. Just be and feel. Content and fulfilled. At peace. Just breathe. Bring your awareness to the natural flow of respiration and breathe every moment full of satisfaction. See yourself grow a smile of contentment and feel a sensation of peace. Breathe. Equally in and out. By breathing a feeling we cultivate the feeling. Within every cell of the body, feel the contentment and satisfaction. All the body is at peace. From the head to the feet. From feet to head.
Breathe and let the satisfaction wander along the body. From the head along the spine to the bottom, below to the feet. Let the feeling of contentment wander from the feet to the thighs to the buttocks. Along the spine up to the chest area, to the shoulders and neck. All fulfilled, all satisfied, flowing to the very peak of the head and to the face. We breathe and create space. With every breathing satisfaction comes and goes. We keep the natural flow. Balance yourself.
Start to observe. The whole world in your breath. All the life that breathes is alive. Even the small pieces and parcels, even the plants and
trees, even the bees and butterflies, even the animals, humans, all beings alike.

All breathing, all alive. Just breathe, be with joy, breathe out. Let it flow. See yourself in a joyful glow of shining golden light. With every breathing expanding. Expand your light from the inside out, from the core to the universe. Breathe. Joy travels with the breath, so see all the beings with this golden light of joy, even in the smallest particle, see the light boundlessly expanding into the world, into the universe. Meet the sun, joyfully shining the light onto the world. See all the world connected to that light and observe yourself in this joyful light. Breathe into this light and be aware of every sensation. Be aware of the natural flow of the breathing. In and out. Every breath connects us to the world, to every being. All the joy is with us, glowing in a beautiful golden light.

See the sun, see the joy, observe yourself and be aware of the balanced breath. In and out, observe, equally in and out. See your family, watch them happily be. Set yourself free and smile. With all the joy, all the happiness.
May all the joy and happiness surround me.
Breathe. Enjoy.
May all the Joy surround me.
Palms together, in front of the chest, let the thumbs touch the heart. May all the joy surround me.
Bow.
Chant and repeat each verse like a call and response, kirtan.
May All the Joy be with All
May all the love be with all
May all the happiness be with all
Love, Peace & Harmony
May all the Joy be with Us
May all the love be with Us
May all the happiness be with us.
Love, Peace & Harmony
May all the Joy be with You

May all the Love be with you
May all the happiness be with you Love, Peace & Harmony
May all the Joy be with me
May all the love be with me
May all the happiness be with me Love, Peace & Harmony
Rest & Relax. Namaste

Self-Confidence Meditation Story

There is a space within the universe where we are all safe and sound. It is the heart of the Absolute Truth, the well-wisher of all beings, as it is the location of the Highest Truth, the one living there is the creator of this universe, with many names and faces, this person gives us shelter in form of a forest flower.

This forest flower is the protection that sits within everyone's heart.
This story my Father always told me, the son Samatura says, smiling and having a glance into the sky, but where is security in the outside world? When I feel insecure, what can I do?

Samatura is now not a little child anymore, he can think and be aware, of certainty and uncertainty. Like us, he knows, there are dangers in the world, but he is brave enough to live a life.
He breathes through and follows the river into the forest where his teacher is situated. 'Sandapa will know, he is a wise man and contributes to the wellbeing of all his disciples and students, but he is more encouraged to share his message of self-aware and peaceful living in this world.

The question of Samatura still roams in his head, where there is confidence in me, there also must be confidence within everyone.
Let's prepare to meet Sandapa, who usually sits under a tree in the forest and writes his scriptures and ancient texts. He is living in the forest for his whole life and never had any fight. Living in security and peace he teaches this message for everyone, especially for the Son of the Kingdom who one day will remain in a position to lead the kingdom to many more generations.

Sandapa awaits the young disciple and son of the Kingdom with a smile. He is very lean and tall, with bright eyes and tender cheeks, his hair is white and he sits under a tree.

'I see you are walking alone from the kingdom, do you think you are free? Bring a friend to come along with you, therefore security will come true.' Sandapa grins and knows all the questions by his disciple. Yet, he invites him to sit for a meditation and we all can join.

Let's find a comfortable position, where we are aligning with the ground and with the sky. Come to ease in that position and gently close your eyes. Let it be like a window opening for the holy altar.

There, on this altar, you see many beautiful deities and pictures of saints, like great masters and mystical beings.

See yourself sitting in this holy place and find ease, watching the candle lights and smelling attractive flowers, so fragrant and nice, the whole room is filled with joy and happiness. It is secure and safe, therefore we don't have to worry about anything. Just breathe, equally in and out, see the air flowing in regularly, and constant, and see it flowing out, regular and constant.

One is safe, to be breathing means to be in the security of life. Here in the body, we are safe, here in the sacred room we are safe, here with a guide and teacher we are safe. Feel the shelter and open your heart, like a lotus flower. Let this lotus flower bloom and see every petal of this lotus flower adjust to the light.

The light shines from your heart and illuminates the room, the petals of the lotus flower open and one is surrounded by this lotus flower light.

Did you know, that lotus flowers even grow in the deepest swamps, where there is hardly pure water and light? Yet, the lotus flower remains unspoiled and graceful in-midst this nature.

Let's go for a soothing and mild walk down the forest lane to find a swamp with many lotuses. There we see the trees opening up a way for Us, the alley leads straight to a little muddy swamp, where we find a wooden floor.

Let's wait here and see the flowers in the distance.

With shimmering silver and purple, the petals of the lotuses surround the yellow golden middle, the stigma. It is a splendid wonder to look at, but how can the lotus flower feel safe in this swamp, so dark and moist?

'It is a wonderful question, let's explore the answer and ask the Lotus flower', Sandapa smiles and plugs a lotus flower, which he will offer to the sacred altar in the room. He knows the answer already but he promises us to bring this lotus flower into a safe place, where he gives it to the other offerings like fruits and milk to the deities. While we return, the Lotus flower starts to speak and gives us many interesting answers to our questions.

In a subtle and clear voice the purple-golden Lotus says:
'I am all attractive, beautiful and kind, as the sunlight comes, I open up. I trust, the sunlight is my benefactor bringing grace and growth.'

As the Lotus explains the ways to come to a place of security we share a human place of security we call home, this home is the place where we find community and joy in the things we do,
 together with our loved ones, we live here, work, study and find attraction naturally.

Samatura is obliged and puts this beautiful lotus flower on his head, 'I will bring this back to my father, so I can tell him everything about attraction, what I learnt today with you. Thank you, kindly accept my humble obeisances.' Samatura bows in reverence and walks on with a lotus flower on his head.

In a beautiful kingdom, that longed to be at peace,
We can explore and walk around the forest at ease. There also is a teacher and when we kindly ask, please.
Give us an answer to our questions, bring us release,
The teacher may illuminate the darkness into light.
As long as there is no fight, we are alright.

Let's enjoy this little bit of life, feel and shine bright.
Even, when we have to say goodbye the day and hello to the night.

As always the day ends, in every wonderful kingdom, and eventually, there comes the night. In this Kingdom, it is a tradition to have a safe and sound ceremony, with oil lamps, and a concert. Beautiful and serene at the same time, the students of Sandapa, as well as the Son of the King, Samatura, are joining the good night ceremony with lights and chants.
Samatura chants:

May all beings be at peace, May all beings find their ease, Shall all live in harmony, Peace, Love and Unity.

The trees are watching the stars, the birds are tweeting their songs, together with the stars that illuminate the night, today there shines a special light, it is a full moon show, with special honour to all the Mothers and Teachers.

There, Mother Nature becomes a special thanks and appreciation, there also all the teachers are handed wonderful flower garlands and presents for their service.
All fits together under the beautiful night sky, the mild wind blows into the trees and makes the leaves start to dance.
There is a chance we see Mataja making a sacred fire, one can sit and see the sacred procession of incense and milk, with flowers and oil lamps, we can also see the holy rivers and streams, that are being honoured and everyone from the kingdom joins together in harmony.
We feel safe and sound on this night.

We can breathe balance and attraction. With every inhale there comes balance and with every exhale we let go of the uncertainty. We inhale attraction and let go of uncertainty with the exhale. Breathe and feel the balance coming to you, and the uncertainty leaving you, more and more we relax and find space to smile.

Let's be happy and celebrate life as it is. Even on this night, there is certainty, tomorrow the sun will rise, as always, we give thanks to our Mothers and Teachers that help us on our path and we thank Mother Earth for Life.

This Lotus flower shines in the most wonderful colours and protects us. The light reaches every part of the body, every cell and we see ourselves in this light, engulfed and surrounded with a healing light of attraction.

Put your palms together and feel the harmony and attraction. Feel good and let the breathing be natural. Like a lotus flower, you can now open your hands and bring them to your lotus eyes. Surround your eyes with the healing energy of the hands and let your eyes bathe in the palms of your hands.

Breathe, equally in and out. Breathe, just naturally.
Maybe sigh, or massage your head, around the eyes and your jaw to feel fine. All is now safe and sound, with a smile we are ready for a good, good life.

www.ingramcontent.com/pod-product-compliance
Lightning Source LLC
Chambersburg PA
CBHW081507080526
44589CB00017B/2681